BASU RAI
from the streets of
KATHMANDU

Edited by
Papri Sri Raman

Vitasta

Let Knowledge Spread

Published by
Renu Kaul Verma
Vitasta Publishing Pvt Ltd
2/15, Ansari Road, Daryaganj,
New Delhi - 110 002
info@vitastapublishing.com

ISBN: 978-93-82711-40-7
© Basu Rai 2014
Reprint 2014

All Rights Reserved.
This is an autobiographical account of a child who grew up on the streets of Kathmandu. This account of the first ten years of his life is as such a mix and match of a child's memories, part his reality, part imagination and is no way related to any other real person's life or events. It could be the life of any child on any street in any city of the world. The views, opinions and quotes expressed in this book are the author's own. The account of his life as a rescued child within institutions like CWIN, Mukti Ashram and BBA and as part of the Global March Against Child Labour are researched and authenticated by these organisations. Basu Rai came to India as a ten-year-old child.

This work is the sole responsibility of the author. The publisher, supporting institutions and sponsors have made a joint endeavor to bring before the world the struggle an abandoned child has to go through on the streets, the opportunity for change he gets through organised support and how, having embraced change, he grows up into a successful young adult.

Typeset & Cover Design by Vitasta Publishing Pvt Ltd
Printed by Vits Press, New Delhi

Dedication

I would like to dedicate this book to all the children who are struggling somewhere in this world and also to those people who with warm hearts give these struggling children a good life and sustaining faith in humanity; such people are very special and without them life would be less humane.

My prayer and wish for those who still believe in humanity and have a kind heart to help the needy and give them a chance to change their lives.

Papri Sri Raman is a journalist and writer, a poet and artist. She has been a Special Correspondent of the IANS news agency for ten years and has worked with *The Indian Express* and *The Statesman* newspapers. With special interest in environment and science, she also writes for the British website scidev.net and is contributing author in a number of books.

৪০ଓ৪০ଓ

Content

Foreword

I feel immense pride in writing these lines for Basu's book. This is a story of millions of children, ruthlessly strewn on the streets as garbage, treated worse than animals, abused and exploited as child labourers. It is a bitter commentary on our insanely civilised world. The book is also a tell tale of strong convictions and sincere efforts to make our society just and humane. It is indeed a story of a cruel joke on childhood, coupled up with innocence, emotions, joy and aspirations.

Basu met me for the first time as a nine-year-old kid in Manila on 15 January 1998; two days ahead of the launch of the world's biggest mass mobilisation in favour of the most deprived children — the Global March Against Child Labour. He was the youngest core-marcher in the Asian lap of the Global March which also had two other simultaneous streams that were flagged off from Cape Town in South Africa and São Paulo in Brazil. I feel blessed to have marched with millions of children like Basu across the world.

Many of those marchers had been interviewed by media about their pains of the past and dreams for the future, but Basu, now twenty-six, is the only one to have put down the recollection of his experiences passionately on paper. Therefore, his book is a reflection of the common miseries, despair, frustration, angst, uncertainty, indomitable survival instinct, unrelenting struggle for existence and identity, confidence, desires and hopes of many of my young co-marchers. Their beautiful faces, sky-ripping slogans for freedom, childhood and education are still fresh in my memory.

It happened all too fast and Basu, from a toddler, grew up to become a smart young lad in front of my eyes, who often shares with me his feelings and emotions, ideas about society and politics, future worries, ambition to become a famous actor, as if there was no tomorrow and his crushes on pretty girls at the drop of a hat. He is a real charmer.

Isn't it incredible that this book is written by someone who was abandoned by his mother when he was barely six months old? He lost his father at the age of four, survived on the streets of Kathmandu and braved the local gangs for a couple of years, was nurtured in a shelter home for about two years before becoming a globe trotter by joining the historic march in 1998. This was nothing short of a re-incarnation for Basu. He got invaluable exposure, self-confidence, friends for life, enormous learnings and experiences that continue to shape his destiny.

I still remember the day when ten-year-old Basu, who ran away from Nepal, appeared at my home all of a sudden. He stayed at Bachpan Bachao Andolan's Mukti Ashram in Delhi for over six years, and then set out to fend for himself on his road to self-discovery, which still continues. Basu was loved and supported as much as he was hated and cheated. His 'Never say die' attitude kept him surging ahead as a fighter who lives his life on his own terms.

This book portrays all colours and shades of his personality, though they appear contradictory sometimes. This makes his story all the more interesting and an inspiring read.

I know how much Basu misses his father because his eyes always keep searching for a father in me, but I was deeply moved when I learnt from his book for the first time ever that he still hopes to find his mother some day and I sincerely pray that he does.

I bless him from the core of my heart.

– Kailash Satyarthi
Founder, Bachpan Bachao Andolan
Chairperson, Global March Against Child Labour

Acknowledgements

It's hard to believe that I'm loved by so many people today, after being an unwanted child; both my mother and society had rejected me, and I was never treated well on the street. I never thought that life would transcend from the gang on the street and show me the light of humanity and love, a far cry from knives and brutal fights to stay alive.

My deep gratitude to my dad, who kept me alive till the age of four.

I'm indebted to Gauri Pradhan who picked me up from the street and sheltered me in his NGO. Because of him, I got a chance to transform into a social child. And thanks to all those teachers and the volunteers who gave me love and always taught the value of being a nice human being. I'm extremely thankful to Kailash Satyarthi who always guided me as a son, such that we always have a candid talk on every subject; and I'm indebted to his NGO, Bachpan Bachao Andolan and the many people involved with it and Rohit Sharma for their inputs; and the many elders and children of the Global March Against Child Labour team, who always treated me as a strong leader and gave me a lot of love, many chances and caring, during my march across twenty countries around the world and thereafter.

My immense gratitude to my friend Dori Santolaya who helped me with my education; Alexandra Sagarra Ballesteros and Alam Rahman, who treat me as their own young brother; and Tilak Pokherel and Chang Ho Chuan, who were always there with support and love. I'm thankful from the core of my heart to my friend, Luis Miranda, who having a warm heart for deprived children, has supported my work, and my publisher, Renu Kaul Verma and editor Papri Sri Raman for their great work. I've learnt a lot from them. And my thanks to Vitasta's team including Alok, Geetali and Megha. My thanks to Moska Najib who contributed the photographs.

I'm thankful to the volunteers from Taiwan, England and America, and those from different universities and many more countries who met me and treated me as their friend and mentor.

ഇൻയെൻയ

Preface

Long roads and crossroads that are endless... time merging into time.

There are many red lights to halt at for a while but after that, life moves on...towards varied destinations and the paths that lead to them.

This Odyssey has a not travelled-before road because it leads to so many platforms of life. Everyone knows what the street is and the road, but there are very few people who really have literally 'gone through the streets'. If you have really travelled through these roads to your own destination, you would have seen many streets, lanes, pavements, bridges, parks, vehicle stops, railway stations and so many other premises and places of temporary halts. These places are not only locations to run different businesses, they constitute the home of various unprotected lives of the populace — individuals called 'the homeless people' or simply bums.

These streets are not just 'spots' to walk around in... there is the very old and neglected world of unprivileged children and so many other homeless individuals, that we never ever think very seriously about. So many lives come here and vanish.

People are not aware of these lives because these streets accept everyone and the street doesn't have any bias, it does not matter where people come from. In these streets, there are many infinitely sad stories of children and many of these children belong to affluent families but because of loveless mothers, fathers, puny hearts of extended family, no willpower of governments to protect them and care for them and unpredictable circumstances, today they are known as 'street children'. There are also the children who are called orphans because of the vicious circle of poverty which starts when parents fall ill and do not have the money to cure themselves. Such people die, leaving uncared for and destitute children on the streets, that's why today we call such children 'orphans'.

Streets contain various kinds of children, like those who have run away from their homes, orphans and children who really have parents around but belong to the slums, these children too spend all day at different junctions and red lights, mostly begging. Like different political parties, the children of the streets belong to different gangs and leagues, and they all live on their own. So, when you see a child sleeping on a pavement, or under the bridge, know that he or she is a 'home runner', or an 'orphan' or someone abandoned as 'illegitimate' by some cruel couple scared of old social norms. Whatever be the manner and whatsoever the reason, the result is, one innocent child gets to be tagged 'orphan'. Actually, we know all about roads and the streets but we are really unaware of the tiny hearts and the feelings of desperation that street children feel because we never ever stretch out our arms to hug, caress and love them.

Today the world has given me many mothers and much love. It is time for me to return it a fraction of that love. I'm not afraid today because my heart says, as the days imbibe the sun's rays on this earth, and the nights are suffused with romantic and lovely moon light, I must spread myself all across the universe, where I will collect many hugs, caresses and mother's love, and at that moment, I shall be known by my name or myself rather than as an 'orphan'.

உ෨ᏣᏒ෨Ꮳ

Too Young For The Street

Memories. Memories of a few words. A few sounds. The few faces I try to remember have faded from my memory. Only faint, shadowy figures still cling on, even the name of the street I lived on is unknown. I don't know which day of which year it was. But the sun was up as I took my new and first tiny delicate step to become a street child, to learn how to survive on the streets.

And I had my first friend. Another street child. I don't remember his name. Only that he had a 'gang' and he gave me protection from other vicious and violent gangs of street children.

My heart ached when I saw the chicken coop. The chicken lived with knowledge of their death and quivered with helplessness. After a while, I just got up and opened the coop and said, 'Come on... run. Get out of here... live your lives...'

Each and every bird ran out of the coop and scattered hither and thither.

My first love, I remember well. I was just sitting and weeping. My gang of friends came looking for me in the rose garden. 'Hey! Basu, you are crying here and your girlfriend is about to go.'

'See...? Pluck one rose from here and directly go on to the stage and kneel down. Then offer her the rose and ask her, if she will be yours?' I plucked the rose as my friend had said, then walked down towards the auditorium.

On hindsight, and recollecting the chain of other people's conversations, I can today tell you it was the city of Kathmandu in the neighbouring country of Nepal. The year was probably 1992, or may have been '93, I don't know exactly which year it was. I was about four years old. I remember:

Every morning, when I used to hear the chirping of the birds, I would wake up and walk down a small corridor, rubbing my sleepy eyes; I would slowly drag a small portion of the curtain aside to peep out through the window and suddenly, when the bright warm sunlight hit my eyes, I would realise that it was time for breakfast!

I would just run to the kitchen to get something to eat. As soon as I had my plate full of food, I would carry it back to my room. There wasn't any choice. My Pop would be lying on the bed, paralysed. I never came out of my room because I was an introverted child and I used to be terribly scared of the people who went in and out of the house. I did not want anyone to see me. I didn't know why at that time, I just did not like to meet people. I sort of hated people and logically, I have never found any reasonable answer for this behavior. As an adult, I love people and I have people around me all the time. I am told, it could be, perhaps because somehow, I believed that I was unfit to be seen by the world, unfit and unwanted. Unwanted by my mother, who had abandoned us. My father and I.

Yes, once upon a time, I lived in a fairy tale house, with my father who I called Pop. It was a long, long time ago. Like you read in storybooks. My beginning was much like yours. Born in a hospital, brought home wrapped in a pink towel. My father was in the seventh heaven of joy. But there was a difference. My mother was in despair. She had carried me for nine months, watching her petite self grow ungainly and 'ugly' in her eyes. Now, after my birth, she quelled at the thought of breast feeding a baby, her beautiful breasts would go flabby. She was born to be a star. She had dreams in her eyes and marriage and baby care had snatched that dream from her life.

Even as a toddler, I knew I was unwanted. My Pop must have told me this. He loved me more than anything else in the world. But he loved me less than he loved my mother. Pop loved me and hated me, because I was the reason my mother had left us. Now, I can tell you all this, analyse all this as an adult. But as a child...no. I did not understand. My puzzlement kept me silent, wondering, introverted perhaps.

But I used to peep out for hours, through the peephole in my room's door, at my father. If there was no one around, I would go and sit with him and talk to him, as he lay sprawled in the living room, on a spacious bed, which must have been the bed he shared with my mother once. He would not give me any answers because he couldn't speak anymore. However, I knew very well that he could hear me, listen to me.

So I used to tell him the same family story which he used to tell me since when I was just six months old. When I used to tell him the same story, I could see his bleary eyes and tears sliding down his cheeks. When the maid came to clean him and the house, I would quickly get up and run into my room. But this story did not last for a long time. I wish that it could have been long-lasting but it didn't happen that way.

One day, I didn't hear any bird chirping, but it was the noise that people were making inside my house. I got up and peeped out through the peephole. I could see that lots of people were around. They were saying something really unusual, but suddenly, I saw my dad's face, which was turned towards my door. So, I slowly opened my door and approached my dad. His eyes were still open. I looked into his eyes for a while. I can't even explain the feelings which I felt at that moment. It was as if he wanted to say something to me. I was just staring into my Pop's eyes. Suddenly, one man said, 'It's okay, son.' Then they covered my dad with a white sheet. I just ran into my room because I was so numb at that time, I couldn't understand what was happening with me. That was the first day that I didn't feel scared of people, but I couldn't stand with them either.

As I got into my room, I locked my door. I just kept peeping out through the spy hole. People tried to open my room but I didn't open it. After sometime, I saw four men pick my dad up and they took him away. The maid just kept on trying to open my room and said, 'Son, open the door. Even your landlord is here.' My Pop had left me to my own fate, to an unknown situation and in the hands of God.

What did I do? I just sat down at my door and missed every care and the love which my father had really bestowed on me, even though it was for a short time. I remembered the story which he used to tell me when he used to be dipso and high; which always reminded me about my Mom, Pop and my own existence. It was not a happy story, though it was like a fairy tale. This story, and my memory of it, gives me the imagination to at least picturise my mother well. I never saw her face, that was not a time when I was grown enough to remember her even vaguely. But it is through my father's descriptions of my mother that I imagined her. And I still do.

In that house, our destinies had been written in each and every wall. Those invisible scripts, which were engraved on the walls of my house were the proof of my birth and the memory of a short-lived and fragile bond. The memory of a family. But with this tenuous thread of being part of a family, I couldn't stop my father from forsaking me and my mother from abandoning me. That home, on lease, was impermanent. When the landlord started to clean every mosaic floor of my house, where I could see the picture of the moments when my daddy used to kiss and play with me, where I could picture his smiling lips as he held me in his arms, I knew something was forever over. Did not know then what an idyll was. But when my landlord's family resettled the furniture and disposed of our souvenirs, I just stood at the corner of one wall and looked at how memories can be erased so easily.

And those walls, walls which really knew the ups and downs of my life, gradually loomed before me and then receded away. So, while touching those sides of walls with my tiny fingers and remembering all that had been, I gradually moved out towards the main door and then the main gate of the house. Then, suddenly, a few drops of tears fell from my eyes. While crying, I raised my right hand up and then waved to the house; then promptly, I turned my head and after that, I just ran without thinking anything. I ran as much as possible, as much as I could. I didn't want to stop. I just wanted to run but my body didn't allow me to run any more. Then I had to stop at one corner of the pavement.

ॐ॰ॐ॰ॐ

The Street Hugs Me

I could speak some words and did not know others because I was very small. The whole of that first day out on the street, I wandered hither and thither. It is strange now to think back. There were so many people on that road, all hurrying to and fro, to reach their destinations. No one asked me who I was. Where I had come from? Where I was going? I just moseyed on the road without any certain destination or intention, just following the long, endless roads and crossroads all day. Gradually, I felt ravenously hungry. It was only then that I really looked around. I saw this one hotel, where people were eating blithely. As I saw those happy faces which were chewing tasty bites of food, I realised that I was drooling and my stomach was rumbling and writhing within. Like a snake that goes into a burrow deep inside the floor, with a smile on my lips, I went inside the eatery and told the owner, 'Good evening, Sir! I'm so hungry. I've not eaten anything since morning and I don't have money either. Could you give me some food to eat?' That whiskery person gazed at me as if I had asked him for his life. He was completely still but his eyes rolled at me, looking me up and down from head to toe. My lips still twitched with a naive smile.

All of a sudden, he shouted at me like a wild animal and charged at me with a scary face, 'This is not some sort of a pilgrim's inn where you get food free. Get out of here!' As I saw his face flushed with rage, I felt terribly daunted. I ran away quickly from that place. It was quite strange. My heart throbbed badly because it was for the first time that someone had shouted at me in that manner. I felt so bad that people didn't love me. I looked right up to the sky and told my Pop, 'Hey! Pop. That person not only shouted at me but he tried to hit me, so you please teach him a lesson.'

I walked along as far away from that hotel as possible, talking to my dad when I saw a beggar who was begging. Now I halted for a while and started to observe him. The way he begged. Then I too swung my head to the left and right, and then recited the same line the beggar was saying. I said, 'Oh! Brothers and sisters! It's been two days since I have eaten anything. Please give me some money. God will bless you.'

It was thus that I became a four-year-old child beggar. When I put out my hand to beg, many people just brushed me off, some bumped at me and passed me by, while some gazed at me very fiercely. The whole day, I just roamed on and on, trying very hard to get something to eat. Unfortunately, I couldn't get a single piece of bread that night. As night fell and it got darker and darker, I got more and more worried. I spoke to myself, 'What should I do now, where should I go? And where am I going to sleep?'

I kept walking and walked on, scared stiff, my heart beating so fast, it was as if a train jangled and roared and my mind was totally blank. I looked hither and thither as I walked and walked. After walking three or four miles, I saw some people were lying down on the pavement. I stopped only then. I searched for an empty spot, then quietly lay down on the pavement, without eating anything. Well... some would say, I was lucky to find a spot to lie down, but my stomach wasn't quite happy with me, it kept sinking as if someone was digging a hole in the ground and my guts were writhing within; as if my guts were going to sink into the ground while I lay crouched down and pressed my belly in. I then started to sob because I was simply too hungry and because, on that first day on the street, there was not a single benevolent soul who was kind to me like my father had been.

People had treated me like a stranger and no one had wanted to take care of me. I did not know then what the definition of a stranger was, I had thought people would help me, be nice to me. I kept talking to my Pop and said, 'Pop, as I understood it, you were going to take care of me. Today I'm terribly, terribly hungry and you are not here to give me even a piece of bread. Papa, help me at least. And please come back for me.' I sobbed quietly, all the while talking to my Pop, but he never even bothered to answer me. Gradually my eyes shut as I lay on the ice cold pavement, sapped of all energy.

ೞಛೞಛ

My First Friend

It was about 1 am in the middle of the night when I heard a voice saying, 'Hey! Get up.' I was still deep in an exhausted slumber. At first, I felt that someone was waking me up. After a while, the voice got louder. I heard someone say, 'Hey, you son of a b..., get up!' Then that someone kicked me. I scrambled up hurriedly. Through bleary eyes, I saw a group of fifteen street children and some of them were drunk. They were older than me and bigger. I was terrified of them. Suddenly one guy came forward and asked me, 'Which gang do you belong to? C'mon...spit it out bastard, why aren't you saying anything?'

I got spooked and wondered what this was all about. I didn't know what the word 'gang' meant. So, in a stammer, I asked the same guy a question, 'Whaa...what do you mean by gang brother?' At first they became quiet. Then, suddenly, they began to look at each other, full of startled wonder. They then began to giggle and said, 'Screw you... scumbag! Are you kidding us? C'mon...brawl the b... nicely! Teach him what is the meaning of gang.' One boy caught me by the collar of my shirt, then picked me up and threw me down hard. I really had not understood what I had done wrong. My legs and hands trembled from fear, but I was so scared that I couldn't do anything to defend myself. By this time, my limbs were not even capable of walking, let alone run or fight to defend myself from those bully boys.

The boys bashed me up pretty brutally. My blood was spilled on the pavement. Some of them had kicked me and some punched me cruelly. Each and every blow was so hard that it shook every bone in my tiny body. The blood running in my vein was cold with fear, and every muscle of my body shook like the tremolo string of musical instruments. They beat me up thoroughly, and then as suddenly, they left me. I had stopped crying as my eyes closed involuntarily and I became drowsy. They might have thought I was dead as I had not spoken a single word in front of them because they had not given me any chance to speak. I had not ever suspected that they were going to bash me up so savagely.

After a while, slowly, I opened my eyes. I looked around and saw that a lot of other boys were sleeping on the pavement. They pretended as if they had not seen anything.

None of them asked me, how I was. It was as if they were already dead and I lay among the dead, the corpses not ready to ask me how I had fared. Gradually, I could feel the pain return to my limbs, each and every muscle in my fragile body ached. I sat frozen, leaning against the pavement wall. Winter had set in and I barely sensed that I was still alive.

I just sat leaning back against the wall, my eyes shut, blinded by tears.

About half-an-hour later, one of the boys came up to me and asked me the same question. Which gang did I belong to? I was so scared, this time I started to beg for my life, groveling and sniveling. I said, 'I am sorry brother, please forgive me... I don't know the meaning of gang, so please don't hit me brother, for God's sake.' I begged him in a pleading, gargling voice. He saw my white shirt, which was covered with fresh stains of blood. My cheeks and lips were still bleeding and clots had formed and my mouth was still filled with blood. He seemed surprised as he saw my state. He said, 'No...No. I won't hit you, don't worry. Are you new on the street?'

I stammered, 'Yes.' Then he twitched his lips and said, 'C'mon...! You got to go to the hospital now.' Then he helped me to get up. Each and every bone and muscle in my body was aching. That boy was so kind that he took me and admitted me to the hospital.

One day later, when I woke up from deep sleep, I just

turned my head right to left and I saw a big clock hanging on the wall which showed 12 o' clock. It was noontime, and I was on a bed. As I again looked around, I could see that there were other injured people too in that room, who were lying on gurneys. The smell of the room wasn't quite friendly and it stank, as if it was submerged in a pond of medicine. Pretty nurses with smiles on their lips were taking care of patients.

While I lay observing the surroundings of the hospital room, I saw a guy heading towards me with a smile on his lips. As he reached my bedside, he said, 'Hi! Buddy, how are you now? Do you remember me? Yesterday you were totally screwed up, so I brought you to the hospital.' The way he spoke was not very decent. But even then, I smiled. I could hardly smile because my lips were still swollen. I answered, 'Of course, brother. I do remember you...and thank you very much for your compassion and you are a great person.' I tried to ingratiate myself before this big boy.

He scoffed and replied, 'What bloody great person buddy?'

'Bloody life is totally rotten, just trying hard to live on this cursed street. In my case, when I came on the street, people beat me up too. There was then one kind-hearted guy who came forward and saved me, even though he was from the street too. So, as I saw you there suffering, I remembered my own childhood. So I helped you.' I was shocked. It was unbelievable that anyone could beat up such a strong guy.

I asked him, 'So, you got bashed up too?' He grinned and said, 'No, not really. I got saved before I died. But you were at death's door. You would have probably died last night. I was luckier than you.' I looked at him, full of fear. I kept thinking, 'How to live in this world?'

In the mean time, Big Brother continued to talk. He asked me my name. I did not remember my name. My Pop had called me 'Son'. From his stories, I knew that he was a Rai and that my mother was a Basu. So I told my big buddy, 'Basu. My name is Basu Rai.'

He again told me, 'Well... buddy you are completely new on the street. And living on this street is the death point sometimes, as you already know. You have gone through the experience of yesterday, so, let me give you some tips on how to survive here.' He explained to me that, 'If you want to survive on this street, you have to join the gang.'

After spending three days in the bed of the hospital, I recovered pretty well. And I was deeply grateful to my benefactor. Had he not been there, I would have been dead. So I caught his hand, to learn to survive on the street. I was a little boy. He was a big boy. Both of us got out of the hospital and I joined his gang. His gang was of pick-pockets and thieves. I was too small to pick pockets or rob or even pick rags, so they gave me a very simple job, which was begging.

In the morning, when a new sun shimmered and beamed its bright light on this earth, when every bird took flight from its nest to search for grub, I took my first step to survive on the street. It was really funny that to live in a different way or in an indifferent place, one really needs to disguise one's self. On the street, you would think, it really doesn't matter how you look or what you are. But, in reality, appearances do matter. You need to appear to be a destitute or a mendicant, or blind. If you want to survive, you really need to know the basic rules and mingle within, so, the first step which my friends took with me was changing my appearance. They got some ragged clothes and they asked me to put these on. The clothes stank horribly. I just could not bear the smell. But my companions laughed. In disgust, I asked Big Brother, 'Why should I wear this shirt, Bro? It's quite disgusting. I think I'm fine with my blood-stained shirt.'

He smiled at me and told me one very simple thing, 'Hey, little Buddy, the first step of life is to get to live. To do this, you have to understand the world. How this world moves. You really need to move according to it. Otherwise you will not be able to survive.'

I was too small to understand this long and tricky sentence, so I asked him again, 'Hey, Big Bro. I really don't get it. What are you trying to say?'

He twitched his lips and said, 'You little Buddy, you

are too cute and very innocent. It is quite a pity that this innocence will not last for a long time. This is the world Buddy! You have to know how to deal with it. The first step, what I'm trying to teach you is, appearance matters. You look very cute but you look like someone from a well-to-do family. You look an elite family kid. So, if you beg, no one will sympathise with you. But, if you disguise yourself and become a pure pauper guy, people will feel sorry and give you money! And that's how, you'll make some money for your survival.'

It was really beyond my understanding then. I was too small to understand the world and at the same time, I was asking myself questions. 'Why should I have to disguise myself? People should understand that I'm alone and I have no job. So, by my logic, they should help me because they are pretty rich folk, richer than me. I don't think they should feel bad to give a few pennies to me.' But I didn't say anything. Just followed Big Brother and said, 'Okay, Big Bro... I really would like to follow your advice because you know better than me.' I put on those disgusting stinky clothes, my new friends tousled my hair and now it looked wild, as if I was a mad kid. Then they asked me, 'Well... this is it...Now you look like a pristine pauper. So, do you know what you should recite while begging?' I immediately told them, 'Yes, I know perhaps!' They were completely startled and said, 'How do you know that?' I smiled and told them, 'Well... when I first came to the street, I saw a beggar who was begging. So I watched him carefully and heard him, how he was really reciting a pitiful babble in front of people, to beg.' As my street friends heard me imitate the beggar, they looked at each other and then giggled loudly. I thought I might have said something wrong. They, however, only said, 'You Little Buddy, you are too smart. We think you'll survive on this cursed street or maybe, you'll be the role model for street kids one day.' Then they all laughed.

Abruptly, Big Brother said, 'Okay, Little Buddy, I think you should start now and we'll keep eyes on you, so there is nothing to worry, right?' I replied eagerly, 'Okay.' We darted towards a place where lots of people were walking around. Some of them were tourists and some of them were local. In that crowd, I was very small. I reached only their waist high, and people bumped into me, some asked me to get aside. I was pushed and jostled from one end to the other. Finally, I thought, I could get aside and so I went into an alley where people were walking around at a less furious pace. There were more tourists here. So I began to beg from them; that day did not bring riches but at least, I did make some money by the time the sun went down.

In the evening, some of my new-found friends took me their home area. It was funny how they lived under a bridge. I was very surprised that they had beds, some food stuff, booze; and some of them sat down and began to smoke weed. They lit a fire, apparently some of them had managed to get some twigs and a bus tyre. So, as they sat around the fire, some of them started to eat, some of them shared the booze around and some lit up their weeds. I sat a little distance away and looked at them. I found them happy and cheerful. As if they had returned home after a long day at work. I had been in a proper home with four walls around me, and the open space under a bridge, filled with clutter...I found it difficult to accept this as home. But then, who cares where home is?

Once they got high, my friends noticed, I was not sitting with them. They missed me and said, 'Hey! Where is the new buddy, man?' I just gazed at them in a surprised way. Suddenly, Big Brother called me, 'Hey! Little Buddy, why are you sitting alone in the corner? Come here, join us man!' First I said, 'No Brother. I'm fine here!' One other guy, who was smoking weed and was probably high, said, 'Hey! Don't say that Little Buddy, you are a part of us now and if we get together, we won't feel lonely on this earth. Otherwise, this world will ball you up badly. On the contrary, if you want to screw these sons of a gun, then join us. We'll bash them up together, right?' Then others started to laugh at him. But Big Brother said, 'This sucker has got wasted completely but Little Buddy, don't mind his words, yeah?' I smiled and replied, 'Don't worry Brother. At least he has the guts and grudge to fight the world but I was the one who got bashed up by the fifteen junkies.'

A boy who's name was Lama, said, 'Don't tell me you got bashed by fifteen junkies?' I replied, 'Yeah! But I wish that it will not happen again.' Lama was completely drunk, and he said, 'C'mon Little Buddy, you got bashed by fifteen people and you are still alive. It means you are like a film hero who can fight with so many villains, you know! So, now onwards, we will call you Hero.' The other boys followed him and said, 'Yes... yes...' Big Brother told me, 'Well...L'ttle Buddy, now you got a new name for yourself, Hero. I think it's not that bad a name, quite nice, rather.'

The guy, who was smoking weed, called out to me, 'Hey! Hero come here man. Just have one puff of it, you'll feel great.' I asked him, 'What is it brother?' He gave me a long look and said, '... I call it "ecstasy" because it gives you the guts to say, balls to the world and live in your own world. So, have a puff, you'll get to know it.' I was wondering what they were really smoking. So I also tried one puff, and then Big Brother said, 'Try one more, Hero.' As I took two puffs, my head went round and round and it was really funny. A few puffs were enough to intoxicate me. The weed master again said, 'Balls to the world.' The other fellows told me to recite after him, so I also said, 'Balls to the world, ba....' My friends did not know I could abuse. They all looked at each other and giggled loudly, and Big Brother said, 'Yes!

That's not bad though. Now you have become a macho man Basu. Good for you.' Then he laughed again. By that time, I had begun to feel very drowsy and my eyes started to shut. I lay down, just where I was and went to sleep.

ഇൻൽഇൻൽ

In A New Avatar

In two-three days, I had two new names. Little Buddy. Hero. Next morning, when I woke up, the same routine started. I had to get to work begging. I was now a professional beggar. I did this job for one long year. Then I started to pick pockets. At the age of five my friends made new plans for me. They thought I looked like a cute little child. No one would ever suspect me. They thought I could mingle in crowds easily and become good at picking pockets. If you do not get caught, it was a very easy way to make money picking people's pockets. There were several children who did this. They said, 'you should try this job, if you can do this, it means you can live life as a prince.' They kept encouraging me to try. Finally, although I was scared, I made up my mind to become a pickpocket.

So they gave me ideas...on how to pick pockets...then they took me in a bus and told me to pick someone's pocket. I tried to do as they said. My hands were shaking very badly and my heart was beating rapidly, I was terribly scared to pick anyone's pocket. My friends were in front of me and some were behind me and some were by my side. Yet I was terrified. Finally, I mustered enough courage and picked up a purse from someone's pocket. And we stopped the bus and got off as soon as possible. We darted from where we had alighted and went to some isolated place, where we could inspect the purse just stolen by me. As we opened it, we saw a lot of money in it. My friend Lama said, 'Let's count how much it is.' Then Lama screamed, 'Holy shit!!!! Its five thousand rupees!!' As we heard this, we freaked out completely and started to jump and holler and the rest of the others began to shout and said, 'Yes!!! We're going to have a party today jerks!!!!!!' They were very happy because it was my first stolen money. That night, we had a party. One of our friends took us into a hotel and we booked a room, and took a bath. Then we had delicious food.

While we were having dinner, one boy spoke up and said, 'Hey! Hero… you did a nice job today and I wish you will do this every day, and one day you will be rich like a prince.' I was very happy with their compliments. So, I chuckled and said, 'Okay… don't worry buddy. I'll do my best, alright?' The others said, 'Cool.'

Then one older friend got serious and in a soft voice, he said, 'Look Basu…you have to be very careful in this field, because here is a matter of your life. It means… if someone catches you red handed…that day will be the worst time of your life. Not only will you get beaten to death by the people…you get me…? But, it's life Bro…got to do this job because you need to survive here, alright?'

I was also very scared by his explanation. I kept quiet, thinking. But I didn't let myself feel depressed or afraid or be defeated. I had made up my mind that picking pockets is what I would do. So, despite the initial hesitation, I continued picking pockets. But as the saying goes, 'The sin overflows the pitcher if it is too much.' I didn't have any teacher to tell me what was right or what was wrong and there wasn't any hand to lead me along the right path. Whatever I was doing at that point of time, whether it was right or wrong, I learnt it from the various critical circumstances. I was just trying to survive on that street, which I had never wished for even in my dreams. Unfortunately, one day I got caught.

It was the day of horror in my life. Well, I didn't know that what I was really doing was sin or was it the right thing to do. My religion was to survive and my worship was to get food for my tiny stomach; it did not really matter to me whether this food came from sin or righteousness. I was about six years old. So, practicing the religion of survival, I became really good at picking pockets.

It was noontime on a bright hot sunny day. I was roaming around, looking for an opportunity to find that one unguarded pocket bulging with money. I had made several attempts that day. But I did not find the right kind of target. Suddenly, I saw a bus jam packed and so, thinking back on my first success, I thought here would be my chance once again and I hopped on to it. As I got in and made my way to the middle, I got crushed between people. I was wriggling and trying hard to get forward, all the while my mind on the pocket I could pick. Then, I spotted a person who was wearing a tight pair of jeans. He had a long purse, half of the purse showed above the rim of the pocket. It seemed to be quite heavy and beckoned to me. 'That's it. It seems I will have good luck today. I'm going to make good money, wow!' So I made my way towards this man, my intended victim, and when I got close enough, I started to gradually pull out his purse. I was looking at him and around like I always did when I was on a job. As I pulled out the purse, suddenly one person from behind bumped into the target. As he bumped the other man, this second man behind me caught my hand. I looked at his eyes and what I saw, made me shrivel in fear. My little hand was in the bigger man's hand and the other man's purse was in my hand. I couldn't think of any further action. I was just paralysed with fear.

I was an expert at my job but even then, when the man who spotted me clutched hold of my hand and suddenly began to abuse me, I was stunned. There were lots of people in the bus. They stopped the bus and dragged me out of it and started to beat me. Everyone was hitting me very hard. Nobody thought anything about such big people all hitting me together. They just continued to kick and punch me, slapping and bashing me with shoes and slippers, whatever they could get in their hands. I began to bleed badly. My mouth filled with blood. I screamed in pain and begged, 'Please forgive me. I am sorry.' But all my pleas fell on deaf ears. No one heard me. I was near fainting. I couldn't see things clearly. I felt giddy and haziness all around; gradually, involuntarily, my eyes shut. I thought, 'I am dead.' Suddenly I heard a voice. 'Are you devils? You are going to kill him…?'

'He is very small. Don't you see?' Then she covered me with her body, trying to protect me from the blows still raining on me. I opened up my eyes and I saw a very old lady who was trying to save me and crying at the same time. I saw her tears, sliding down her crisscrossed, wrinkled cheeks. Yet human beings had turned into devils for those minutes, they wanted to kill me like savages, such was their anger. It was only when the old woman kept hugging me, sheltering me with her body that gradually, one by one, every one stopped hitting me. They then all climbed back into the bus. They kept asking the old lady to climb in too, as the bus was ready to move. The conductor of the bus called out to the lady but she didn't get into it. The bus soon left.

The lady stayed on the road, still cradling my head in her lap. She kept wiping the blood from my face. Then my eyes closed. I do not recall anything more. I could have fainted. When I became conscious, I found myself, once again, lying in the gurney of the government hospital. This time two police officers sat by my bedside.

At first I was very surprised and said, 'Oh Gosh! Is this real? Am I still alive? It's a miracle.' But, at the same time, I was acutely aware that two policemen were sitting beside my bed. I thought, 'Holy shit! I'm in trouble again.' So I just tried to move my hand but I couldn't because it was aching and badly swollen. I made a little moaning sound. One policeman looked at me and said, 'So, young man. You got nicely bashed up today, isn't it?' And they began to laugh at me. I was terribly frightened. Shaking from top to toe. At the same time, I was thinking, God helped me by sending that old lady to save me from a mad and savage crowd of adults.

The cops made me get up from the gurney and they took me to the police station. As I reached the police station, they made me sit in an armchair and asked me, 'Okay, tell us for how long have you been picking pockets?' As they began to question me, I felt more frightened. 'Oh God! It seemed that I have messed up completely.' One cop again repeated the question, 'Hey! Scumbag. I don't have lots of time to bang my head, so it would be good for you if you tell me right straight, now, for how long have you been emptying peoples' pockets?' I promptly replied in a stammering voice, 'S...s...sir, it's been a month.'

One policeman came to me and pressed my hand and asked me, 'Do you feel pain?' I started to scream and another police officer said, 'You nasty crap. I don't want to see you around the street anymore and if I catch you red-handed again, think that you are dead, understood?' I was quivering and replied quickly, 'Yes, Sir. I won't do it again. I swear!' As I said this, he nodded and said, 'Okay. Just piss off from my sight now, otherwise you'll be behind the bars. C'mon get lost now!' He allowed me to get out of the police station. I was so frightened by the cops that I forgot that I was in terrible pain. So I just got up and hit the door, and limped out of the door as fast as I could.

Then I stumbled to the familiar bridge. I lay down under the bridge on a sack. It took great effort because every muscle of my body was cramped and in great pain. As I touched ground slowly, it seemed my body was on fire. I screamed out in pain. I looked up at the bridge and heard vehicle sounds, which were passing overhead in a continuous stream. My tears fell as I stared up above at the underside of the bridge. I remembered my father. I missed my Pop a great deal. I felt all alone. There wasn't even a single friend around me. I found myself lonely and deserted. I wept and cried loudly. I rolled my eyes at the sky above and asked my Pop, 'Hi! Pop. Where are you? I need your help. Please come and caress me. I'm in a lot of pain today. So I need you father!' But my father. He never came. I just kept talking to my father. I kept saying, 'I am suffering a lot Papa. No one loves me here on this earth. Every one hits me and I cannot do anything to protect myself. I'm not capable of helping myself. You know what Pop?'

'You are so bad that you left me alone and vanished. How could you be that mean Pop?' But there wasn't anybody to give me any answers. I just kept talking but I did not get even a single response. Then I started to think about that old woman who saved my life. I used to hear about God. So I thought, God might have sent her to protect me.

I still think about her.

Who was she? Why did she appear, to take such kicks and punches on my behalf? Why had she wept for me? Sometimes, I do ask myself a question. 'Was she an angel?' Because she appeared as an angel for me, it might be God's plot that he wants me to suffer a lot on this earth. Therefore, he didn't let me die.

At night, some friends came to me and tried to lift me up. I screamed so loudly in pain when they touched me, that they were startled. They asked me, 'What happened?' I told them the whole story about public rage and how people had beaten me mercilessly. It was a winter evening. So, some of the boys lit a fire and warmed up. One older buddy said, 'Hey! Bro... Next time this will not happen because I will give you a weapon to defend yourself, alright?'

I recovered after two weeks. My friend gave me a very sharp knife. This incident made me a very strong lad; I felt very brave. I was no longer scared. I thought, if people attacked me, I could kill them with my knife. I acquired a do-or-die kind of bravado. I had the feeling and understanding that I could do things which my older friends couldn't do. I became so violent after that — that I would not hesitate to thrust my knife at anyone.

One day, there was a curfew in the city. That day was unfortunately a very bad day for us. There was not a single bus or vehicle plying. There was no one on the road. I and my friends remained under the bridge. Some were smoking drugs and some were playing cards. I was just sleeping. At night, we were very hungry. We had starved all day and by evening the rumbling in my stomach was like thunder. Finally, we decided to get out of the bridge's underside and search for something to eat. We didn't have a single penny in our pockets. Even then, everyone started to search frantically, and turned their pockets inside out; but no one had anything in their pockets. Everyone said, 'Godda… it! Didn't get even a single bloody penny.' I didn't have to curse because I was still fumbling in the inside pocket of my pants and sweatshirt. I found a hundred rupees from inside my sweatshirt pocket. Everyone was so excited. They screamed and said, 'Yes Bro! This will be of great help for these empty stomachs… to live through this long night. Thanks…Basu.'

I had the money, so we planned to go to some place to eat something. Suddenly, some dopers saw us and started to threaten us to give up the money. They were much bigger and more robust than us; I would say they had well-built physique. In front of them, we were just puny little creatures. One guy said, 'Hey! You guys are not going anywhere till you take out the money from your pockets, c'mon! Well… take it out, whatever you guys have; hurry up! We don't have time for negotiation.' Abruptly, I spoke up. I said, 'Hey bros… today we are starving, so we got to eat something. Come tomorrow, we'll give you two hundred rupees, alright?'

One guy spoke up, 'You little punk; don't fri…...try to be so smart, yeah, otherwise I'll bloody kill you right here. Now come on…! Give us the money.' They suddenly started to push and kick us. They snatched my money and then everybody was beaten by them. I was very angry. I got up and screamed very loudly, 'You son of a …! You'll be sorry for your birth; you nasty piece of a shit!' I took out the knife from the sheath and shoved it into the doper's stomach. But I was too small. As he moved away, it was at his waist that I drove the knife into. He started to scream so loudly that all his friends, the other junkies, charged at me to kill me. However, my friends were also around and some of them had knives too. A melee ensued in which everyone had knives out which were shoved into whosoever they found them.

The junkies were yelling with pain; but in the meantime, we also ruffled their pockets and took out whatever money they had, so that's how we made a thousand bucks that night. It suddenly started raining. I was still kicking those guys in extreme anger, like some savage little animal. However, some of my friends pulled me away and said, 'Leave them Basu, we got to go now. We'll take care of these scumbags next time.' Then we ran to our secret hotel, where we went daily to eat. As we sat down on the chairs, we took a long breath.

Some of my friends were breathing heavily. The fight had been sudden and fierce. It had ended abruptly. We had run away. One of my friends finally spoke up. He said, 'Oh! Heck man! Our clothes are all wet. What the heck do we do now?' Lama replied, 'Well.... I don't think God is very happy with you buddy; it's raining outside and our clothes are also wet.' Everyone was chuckling. In the meantime, the waiter came to us and asked for our food order. Big Brother said, 'Hey! Basu, are you bleeding or what?' As I looked at my shirtfront, I saw blood patches splashed on the shirt front. I immediately opened my shirt to explore, if it was blood from any injury to my body. But I didn't see a single scratch on my body. I scoffed and said, 'Thank God, nobody stabbed me!' My friends were looking at me with concern. Lama said, 'Well... Basu don't worry. You are alright, it's not your blood luckily; it's the blood of those idiots.' Abruptly Kumar banged the table, 'Yes! It means, we scr…ed them nicely.' Big

Brother replied, 'Yes! That's what I'm talking about. Now let us eat. I am ravenous. We got enough money today, so tell me whatever you want to eat.' I said, 'Brother. I would like to have Chow Mein and tomato soup.'

೭೦ಛ೭೦ಛ

Sleeping On Salt

After having a nice dinner, we moved out of the hotel, burping. As we got out of the restaurant, all of us were drowsy. So we headed towards a neat and clean pavement, planning to sleep on the pavement that night. But it started raining heavily again. So we scattered in different directions once again, in search of some dry night shelter. I was just walking on the pavement lined with shops. Suddenly, I saw this big grocery shop where stacks of salt sacks were lying, covered with large plastic sheets. It was a huge pile, as high as a single-storey building, it seemed to little me. I climb on it and entered under one of the plastic covers, curled up and tried to sleep. I spent the whole night on that stack of salt sacks.

It was a horrible nightmare. I thought I would be dead by the morning. I was so cold and absolutely frozen. It was raining and it was a cold winter night. I couldn't sleep due to the freezing cold. I just crouched under the sheet, my head on my knees and tried to go to sleep but those salt sacks were cold like ice slabs. I was exhausted and unnerved by the fight; somehow, my eyes closed even as I shivered.

It was only in the morning that I woke up. I couldn't even stretch my limbs, my backbone had bent, my whole body was frozen. I could literally hear my bones cracking as I straightened. As I fumbled in my pocket, I found some money in it. It was very noticeable that my body was numb with cold. However, I forced myself to straighten. Gingerly, I moved towards a tea stall. Finally, slowly, I sat down on a chair. But my words were jumbled and equally frozen as I asked for a glass of tea. 'Can you give me a glass of very very hot tea please?' After having a glass of tea, I felt a little better and my body got a little warm. But I kept thinking, 'Why don't I have a home?'

I soon got up from the chair and ambled ahead. All the while, as I walked along, the running thought in my head was, 'Why is this world so full of bias and discrimination? Even God creates differences between people. Why do some people have lots of things, and some do not have anything? Why do some people get lots of happiness and some have to always cry? Why do some get lots of love in their share and some get stream of tears?' As I ambled along aimlessly and with emotions overflowing, suddenly I heard the ringing of bells.

I swung my head around, I could see the temple and the bells, which were ringing. It was as if the bells were calling out to me. I veered and I moved slowly towards the temple. As I walked into the temple, once again I began talking to God. I do not remember where and from whom I had first heard the word 'God'. Or how I had gathered the idea of God. But I knew, there was someone up there called God. God had a home. A house. Many houses. So, often, I spoke to this God. I said, 'Hey! God. You snatched away everything that was mine. Instead of giving love and happiness, you have given me a lot of pain. At least give me a home to protect myself.' But this God never heard me, because, in this world, God also hears those who really have a lot of resources and who always admire God. I was the one who was always fighting with God. I didn't have the wherewithal to propagate his name to the masses and sing his glory. I was always critical, demanding of him. I kept complaining to God about God. All this was not very coherent. As an adult, I am trying to give expression to my thoughts then, I have words now. A six-year-old did not have the words. God was someone up there. However, I had a righteous feeling within me. I do not know how it came. I do not know what it meant then. But I had a sense of the wrong and the right. So, this time, I thought, 'I'll do something. I will do everything but not pick pockets any more.'

I looked at the temple. Then I walked out of the temple. I walked around aimlessly all day. I did not try to pick anyone's pocket that day. I just loafed around all day. And I spent all the cash I had and didn't do anything. Gradually, the day turned dark and I moved under the bridge where we daily met, me and my friends. That bridge was like our home because every day, in the evening, we would all gather here, under it. We would sit around a fire. We would burn any tires we could find to make the fire and keep ourselves warmer and cosy. In the evening, in the darkness, our stray lives were lit up by this fire under the bridge. We came home to our friends. Our gang. On this day, I was the first to arrive. I sat waiting for the others to come in. My friends were all surprised because I reached earlier than them. So, one of them asked me, 'Hey! Basu, you are so much more quicker than us. You must have made a lot of money today isn't it? C'mon buddy! Let's have a tally of it.' My friends were looking at me, with smiles on their lips and happy faces. Their faces were full of anticipation. They thought they would have lots of money from me. I looked around, and then, lifting my head, I said, 'I have quit picking pockets and now, I would like to do something else in life.'

Everyone was astonished. Finally, Lama said, 'Are you crazy or what? You are pretty trained in this task. You won't be able to do any other job. Do only this.' I said, 'No. No... I will do something else. I will not steal any more.'

Kumar said, 'Alright, then you can change your job now. But it will be more difficult and harder than this. You have to do a lot of struggle, work till the evening to earn some money.

And it's not respectable and happy work. Even nasty, stray dogs may run behind you, bark and perhaps bite you too. So, are you ready for that?' I replied very happily, 'Perfect! But tell me, what is the job that I have to do?' Everybody grinned at me and said, 'You know, what? You are the most imprudent lad on this earth.' Another friend, named Boka, spoke up then and said, 'Fine. Then do whatever you desire to do, alright? So, tomorrow onwards you can join me and we can both do the same work.'

Suddenly I heard the announcement in the airport, as I returned from my flashback trip. I could see the hustle and bustle of people around me; and my facilitator appeared before me and said, 'Hey! C'mon! Be ready! We need to board the plane.'

ജാൽ‍ജാൽ

Taking Wings

*M*y limbs quivered in excitement. My heart beat pitter-patter, like rain. I kept thinking and thinking, over and over again, 'How would this airplane take off? If it crashed, I will be dead.'

My head was filled with ridiculous thoughts. It was the first time that I was boarding an airplane!

Finally, we got into the plane and I could see there were many people inside. People were looking for their seats. Others were already seated. Some were black and some were white. Some were tall and others short. I could see a variety of people in that plane but I felt calm once I saw the air hostesses. They were very pretty, like angels and dolls. I too felt brand new. I felt like a small baby bird, like a little bird out of the nest and taking a long flight. That first flight in wonder. To see the unseen. I had realised that the world wasn't as small a place as the one I was living in. It was filled with many many things from which I'd been very very far.

My eyes suddenly spotted one family where children, a husband and wife were very happy. They were talking amongst themselves. I could see the mother kissing the child and saying, 'My baby' and singing to the baby. A deep desire then emerged inside me and my mind said, 'I would be happy today if my mom and dad had been with me.' There was a bonding in the family on my flight that I saw and felt and could connect with. The feeling of being loved, being wanted. So, I smiled and sat down and fastened my seat belt. Then I closed my eyes. I wanted to think about my Pop. I wanted to imagine my mom. I went over again and again all that my Pop had told me about my mom. It was a lullaby I had grown up with. I had heard this same story — my mother's and my father's love story, every day of my life, as long as I had lived with my Pop.

ॐ☙☙ॐ☙

The Rise Of A New Moon

*M*ost *children in this world have parents. I have heard parents are like 'God' because they give life or birth to us. I know, I also had parents, like all other children. I understood that my father belonged to India, with a family name Rai. But I could be mistaken, though I think I am not. I do not have any information as to which part of India did he really belong to. And I know my mother belonged to Dhaka, the capital of Bangladesh. With a surname, Basu. This name too is in my thought. How do I know this story? I am an orphan. I am a child who has grown up on the streets. I, somehow, always knew this story. It was within me since my waking moment. The eternal love story of man meets woman. And here I am, Basu Rai.*

And this is how I remember it. This is how I retell it for you:

My Pop was pretty handsome, six feet tall, social in

nature. He had a flashing innocent smile. He was educated and a gentleman. He was well-to-do and he loved to attend lots of parties. He was, what one would call, a jolly good guy. The world was his friend and he was a friend to whomsoever he met. He accepted strangers as his own. How do I know all this? It is in my mind's eye, since I can remember. The picture of my tall and handsome father I can and do remember. I wish I could take it from my mind and print a photograph of the image I have of him. His life was full of joy and the bliss of giving, sharing and caring. He was always among friends. Even if it was not true, if you ask me, I would only like to have a positive image of the father I don't have. I wouldn't have it any other way.

My father was the life and soul of parties and parties were his life and soul. My father thrived on parties. He loved other people's voices. He loved to meet different people. He loved to listen to their stories, especially when they had downed a few pegs and bared their souls. Drunk, people laughed, cried, blurted out many truths. He listened to each and every story carefully. And, there was one other thing. Whosoever the girl my father was with, he would love her unselfishly. Yet, it was important for him to fall in 'love'. He was looking for his ideal woman. One night, he found her, dancing on the floor, at a party they were both at. This has happened to you. This can happen. It can be just as much a reality as it is an imagined notion.

My father was party hopping, when he spotted the charming woman, fleeting from one dancer's arm to another. It was at a bar. In some Indian city. At first sight, Pop could not control the beating of his heart. Instantly, he made up his mind to meet the woman of his dream. My Pop was actually very innocent and shy. He found it difficult to approach women or talk to them. So, going up to his dream girl was like moving a massive boulder for him. I understand the feeling. The worry, the hesitation. Won't she, will she? It happens to many of us guys. It happens to me. So I understand it, though, I may not be able to quite explain it.

So, Pop tried very hard to approach her and speak to her. After several attempts, he did manage to speak with her. But his heart throbbed, his voice muffled, his hands shivered. It was as if he had just weathered a blizzard. But then, love is love! You know! Nobody can stop love if you have strong love and conviction. On the other hand, you need to express love too. My father just saw her face. For him, it shone like the moon. A full moon, full of light, a glowing smile on her face. She was simply too cute. She was dancing, her lustrous hair waving and swinging around, it made my father so restless and drove him mad. As he got closer to her, he kept looking at her — the dream girl — her hair flying and the her fragrance spreading its magic charm over my father. He was already dreaming of burying his face in her dense long hair; he tried to say, 'Hi!' But it was really funny that my

Pop's voice did not come out.

Pop was in love. He could not just leave without saying a word. His heart was aflame with love and so his resolve was stubborn. This made him talk to my mother again. She was dancing and continued to whirl by. He got close to her and said, 'excuse me'. She stopped moving. With surprise writ large on her face, she turned around to confront my father and said, 'Yes, may I help you?' Pop just continued to smile at her and gazed at her like a fool. When she looked straight at him, stammering, he said, 'Actually... Miss...uh... are you alright?'

My mother was startled. Then she detected the concern in his voice and said, 'What happened to you? I'm fine.' She giggled and smiled, and then turned around and got on the floor again. As my Pop saw her smile again, he went completely crazy. He jumped up and down, following her and then in a freak moment, shouted, 'Yes! I got her. She likes me!' He shouted so loudly that everybody looked at him. So did my mother.

But she smiled and asked him, 'What was that?' My Pop replied, 'Actually Miss... I... uh... I'm a fan of your dancing. I mean... I like your moves... No, no. Sorry... I didn't mean that. Actually, I like you so much.' As she heard his words, my mother suddenly felt shy. She said, 'Okay. You like my moves, huh?' My Pop was very embarrassed by his own bashfulness. He closed his eyes and said, 'I love you!! That's it, and I'm sorry... If you feel bad about it, please forgive me.'

My Pop's eyes were tightly shut. He was just standing in front of her. She smiled and said, 'So sweet! I love the way you proposed.' Then she caught my father's hand. Pop opened his eyes and he could see this pretty girl standing in front of him. He had really liked her at first sight and he had just given his heart away. The best part of it was, she was holding his hand. Pop just smiled but couldn't say anything. He was as shy as a girl. He bowed his head and said, 'Can we go out? Can we talk in private? Well... if you don't mind?' My mom smiled at my dad and said, 'I like the way you feel shy. So much sweetness inside you, you don't need to be embarrassed. I have already taken your hand. So, let's go out.' My Pop raised his head and said, 'Thank you so much. Actually, it is the first time in my life that I have proposed to a girl. And it really worked! So... let's get out of this crowd.' As my father began to cut across the crowd, to get out, holding my mother's hand, his friends crowded around. It was the very first time that my father was going out with a girl. One of his friends, a little high and with a glass of wine in his hand, came close and said, 'Hey! My friend, it is awesome that you got a nice girl. And you, ma'am! Don't ever leave him. He is a very nice guy and I know he'll give you so much love.'

My father was blushing. He flushed and smiled and said, 'Don't listen to him. He is a little drunk.' My mother smiled and said, 'let's go out then.' My Pop supported her and said, 'Yes. Let's go.' It was so strange. A party was going on. People were coming and going. My father and mother had no place to sit. So they decided to sit on the stairs of the bar and then began to share things. Pop was new to this. So he said, 'would you like to know about me? Or would you tell me something about yourself?' My mom said, with a full smile on her face, 'You go first.' My Pop got trapped. He smiled and said, 'Well... don't know what I should say. But please don't mind, if I say something which you don't like.'

My mother liked the way my father spoke, his style of courting her. She told him, 'You can say anything, I'm not going to mind, all right?' When she said this, my father picked up greater courage. He now opened his mouth and spoke directly to my mother. He told her, 'Actually, what I want to really say first, is ... I really liked you at first sight. And I'm telling you, I gave you my heart at first sight.'

He then said, even without a pause, 'Now, if you don't mind, I would like to propose marriage.' My mother was terribly shocked. In her young life, nobody had ever proposed marriage, nor said, he loved her in the way my father did. My father had just met her. She could have just been his one-night stand. But he wanted to make her his life partner. My mother was stunned. She just could not believe this was happening.

'Well...right now, I'm thinking of becoming a super

model. I'm struggling very hard for that. I have never thought about marriage or that it could be so soon.' My father said, 'Actually, I want to be a reputed businessman. And you want to be a super model. So, our lives are full of struggle. Why don't we get together forever and help each other?'

I don't know what my mother saw in my father, that she accepted his proposal and said, 'Well... I'm struggling here in India, for a long time. I have never had a good friend so far. Today, I have got a life partner who has a heart full of love for me. It's really unbelievable.' As my father heard her yes, he jumped up like a child and said, 'Yes! I have found my love!' He shouted so loudly that people who were around were startled and grinned at him, and thought he was insane. My mother just looked at him and wondered at the intensity of his love. This was the man she was going to marry.

Suddenly my father caught my mother's hand and said, 'Let's go in and dance together.' My mom was laughing and covering her face with both her hands. My Pop was flying in the sky. He was in love. He promptly asked her, with a mischievous smile, 'My love. Would you dance with me tonight, for the beginning of our happy life?'

ॐ☾ॐ☾

Waking Up

My father behaved as if he knew my mother from a previous birth. My mother could not resist his enthusiasm and charm. She sat on the stairs and laughed with him, aloud and happy. As my mother rose, my father pulled her hand and ran to the dance floor. Then they danced around like two insane people, twirling round and round, whirling in each other's arms. My Pop was so happy, he could not control his happiness and he danced in joy. His friends kept looking at him and wondering. Actually, my father was a good dancer. My father and mother danced together all night. This magical night made them my Mom and Pop. Their friends encouraged them. After this first crazy night, my mother and father started meeting each other daily. She was from Bangladesh and a very pretty woman; a minor model too. He was crazy about her, she was very beautiful. He wanted to marry her at once.

However, both of them feared the caste and clan systems in India. My father belonged to the Rai clan and my mother was a Basu. Also she was not Indian. She was probably in India without valid papers. So, like two immature lovebirds, my mother and father ran away to Kathmandu, the capital city of neighbouring Nepal. They got married and after a year, suddenly, one miracle happened. I was born.

My mother didn't want a child because she wanted to be a super model. Her dream seemed to have shattered the moment she conceived. In regular cases, each and every mother on this earth breast feeds her baby, be it a wolf mother or human mother. My mother didn't do that. She did not want to breast feed me. She felt, that would spoil the shape of her breasts. Childbirth itself, she thought, was a process that would spoil her figure. She was angry. Angry with my father perhaps. That marriage with him had led to this. May be, she was angry with the world. This was how things were for her. Not the way she had dreamt. I had not done anything. I was just a living little body, born on this earth accidentally. Yet one thing always knocked at my heart. The feeling that, 'The mother who kept me inside of her womb for nine months, how could she hate me so much?' At those moments my heart gave me just one answer. Its said, 'May be, there is the phrase: fate exists in this universe.'

When I think about the word 'fate', however, I think of the writer or creator. Who makes or creates this fate? Is that really God? If he is really creating human destinies, then why does he discriminate against me? I was also a child. I also had a small heart beating inside me. What should I tell myself? Should I tell myself that, 'No, no. Actually God is great because whatever he does, he does it for the right.' Or should I pacify myself with the fact that I wasn't in God's list.

Well... I don't really believe in destiny. So far, whatever has happened to me, it is because of my daily endeavor and effort. I've learnt to take some hard toddler steps and taught myself to march ahead in life. Once, I could hardly fill my stomach, I found the mean streak in this world and I could not defend myself from kicks and blows.

Yet, I know one thing. It is my unshakable belief that the true writers of one's destiny are parents. It all depends on what they do and how they write our fates. I am a rare case. I have been unwanted from Day One. Unwanted by my mother. Right from the beginning of my birth one word that has been written on my destiny is a 'griever'. One who is always grieving. Always sad. I grieve for everything: love, affection, a mother. A mother's care and I grieve that I have no daddy to hold my hand and let me walk with him.

My case was unusual in yet another way. My mother hated me. Did not even feed me. But my father loved me. He took on the role of the mother. He bottle-fed me. He changed my *diapers. He played with me and sang to me and he told me stories. He told me the greatest story on this earth. The story of how he loved my mother.* Whenever my mother nagged him, he smiled and apologised to her. Pop used to love her a lot. I can today say, he loved her implicitly, he was ready to sacrifice everything, give her everything. He even gave up contact with his family for her. He loved her more than he loved me. I can proudly say, my father was a person who was meant for love. He loved my mother from the beginning to the end of his life.

But her intention was terrible. My mother wanted to take all his money and wanted to leave me forever. She was pretty confident of her action and a very daring woman. She had all the bank accounts in her name. She used to have a different foreign account, without the knowledge of my Pop. One day, my father was out of home, away for a weekend business trip. That day, finding opportunity, my mother took all the money and ran away. She left me at a bus stop. Alone. I could crawl. I was less than a year old.

I started to cry. I could not find my mother or any familiar face. After a minute or so, I crawled down under the wheel of giant bus that was stationary at the bus stop. I was just searching for a place to hide. I was totally unaware of the bus or that the wheel could move. Look at my luck! Suddenly, one traffic policeman saw me and dragged me from underneath of the bus. He was swift. Otherwise, the bus would have run over me. After that I was in police custody. At the same time they thought, the best way to send a message to the family of a lost child was to give an advertisement on television regarding a missing baby. As the news flashed on the television screen, my father got to see it. He recognized the baby in the picture and rushed to the police station. He was completely numb. He did not know how I had got there. Nor where my mother was.

When he brought me home, he realised what must have happened. He also soon realised that he was completely broke. He could not figure out what he really wanted to do. For a few days he just sat on a rocking chair and looked out of the window. His eyes were frozen and his body was completely cold. It was as if he had lost himself in the darkest storm on a winter night. The man was in deep doom, lonely and numb. He kept gazing at me as if a statue was gazing at me. His eyes did not blink. His eyes had frozen. He did not notice if I was weeping silently or crying aloud.

ೞೞಣೞಣ

Beginning Of The End

It was the turning point of my Pop's life and mine too. This is when he started to drink.

He started to drink. He stopped working. He would shed copious tears for his lost love. At that time, I was too small to even remember how it was, what happened. From then on, till about when I was four years old, my father would always curse me. At the same time he caressed me and loved me. He cried to me. He laughed before me. He used to tell me the whole story of my mother and his love affair, every day of our lives together. Every day he would tell me the same story till age four. Most other children, that age, hear lullabies and go to sleep but I was different. My lullabies were the stories of my family. I got the whole story about my parents, from my Pop, even before I could speak. I heard it every day. And so many years later, in my head is the image, although much faded, of a father and a son. A father crying and telling a story. The story of his biggest love.

May be he knew very well that when I'd get older, I'd wonder who I am, I would search for an identity. What he forgot was to tell me his own name and that of my mother. It is true, no one tells a one-year-old child, his mother's name is Meena or Rina or Shanta or Kanta. No one tells a one-year-old, his father is Raju or Ram or Rohit or Roshan. My father was quite intelligent. But he forgot to tell me his name. He forgot to tell me my mother's name. Instead, he drilled into me, their love story. How they had met. How they had danced. He died and left me at the age of four, having fed a fairy tale into my head. But this was vague, including my mother's name and his own name. I know just his surname and mom's last name, because my Pop wanted to create a name by their own surnames only. So I got my name, Basu Rai. Basu is the surname of my mother and Rai is the surname of my father. He did not think that for the rest of my entire life, I would remain the son of nameless parents.

When my Pop died, I didn't even cry, I couldn't understand yet why? I wasn't so emotional at that time. I can only say that at that time, I was unaware what it was to be dead and what it was to be alive. I could only see his eyes, which had been like stones and which had glared at me. I too had stared into his stationary eyes. I don't know what my father really wanted to say in the end, but those motionless eyes were saying something; as if he was attempting to apologise to me and he might be regretting the fate and destiny he had left me.

I couldn't understand what was really happening out there. I just watched, with curiosity and helplessness. People kept coming and going but I didn't stop to look into my Pop's eyes. I had already seen the glistening of tears on his cheeks, a faded streak, almost dried out. But I was never able to forget his lips, which had twitched slightly, as if he was smiling at his fate and mine. People say, when people die, they don't talk because the soul leaves the body but when I had looked at my Pop's eyes, I felt that he was talking to me. I sensed that he was saying, 'Sorry son, I couldn't do anything for you. I was so selfish that I lived my life just for my love. I almost forgot you. But my son, you have to live and struggle for your life on your own. I will not be there to hold your hand and show you the path, so you just need to figure it out on your own. Somewhere, from heaven, I'll be watching you always. So son, try not to become the rolling boulder. You flow along and it means you lose your existence and your own identity, so always remain what you are — a humane person with a loving heart. So all the best of luck for your life, my son!'

People surrounding me then told me, 'He is dead.' But I couldn't understand why they were saying that, because I had felt, his eyes were saying lots of things to me. Some I could understand, some I couldn't. It is strange how people say a lot of things through their eyes, even when they do not utter a single word. But their eyes talk. A heart understands such unspoken and unheard words. Actually, if you really try to understand people through the heart it would be very difficult, unless you yourself understand your own heart first. We all pretend to understand people's feelings. But actually, we don't really understand. I recall, when my father died, there were some people, who kept smiling and talking. Some others, who had cared for him, shed a few drops of tears. But in reality, no one cared what happened to him or his son. No one missed me when I walked out of that house. People only care about themselves.

It is up to a person, how he understands others. One has to be acquainted with the language of the heart, otherwise it would be really difficult to perceive the feelings of distinct hearts, because only a heart knows, how to give love. It really knows how to erase pain. It really knows the right path to take. That's why pure scholars always try to tell you that follow the heart, you'll never be wrong, because your existence is telling you to do that. So, you wouldn't be wrong in any case, if you lost something by following your heart. It means you really follow humanity. Some people like to accumulate wealth but what is the use of it, if you are not satisfied by your own action? That's why, the Bible says, 'You'll be judged the same way as you judge others.'

Every action has a resonance. It's up to you, what you really want back from your actions.

Infinite human beings come on this earth and depart, but there are some people who really understand the meaning of arrival and departure from this world. So, whosoever really recognises the meaning of advent, they utilise it and give something to this world, and in return, the world also doesn't forget them, it keeps them alive or illuminated forever, but whosoever does not realise the coming or going away, they just appear and then vanish, nobody remembers them. So it is inevitable that once you are born, you indeed have to die too.

But whosoever is the real human being, they try hard to sustain themselves and try to become immortal, and if they suffuse this earth with love, this world loves them eternally. When you take birth, everyone around laughs, but you are the only one who cries. When you die at least, everyone should cry for you, but you should be the one who smiles and goes away.

Light — 'tis within me and the catastrophe streaming around me is déjà vu. I have crossed many worlds to come to this earth. I'm scrambling on this earth, though there are no eyes that can see it. So, like flotsam which float away in a flood, I too vanish from sight. But there is a light of hope which flickers inside of me and a thought that, 'One day, I will butt the sea shore and the light within me will be observed. Then this universe will give me a heart full of love.'

Abruptly, my chaperon shook me, because it was time for the plane to land. I also heard the voice from the speaker saying, 'May I have your attention please. The plane is going to land shortly. Please fasten your seat belts.' As I looked down to fasten my seat belt, I saw it was already fastened. When I looked out of the window, I could see Hong Kong, looking all dressed up and pretty.

ഇൽരൂഇൽരൂ

My Campaign Begins

*T*he airport looked like it was situated in the middle of water and its lights twinkled gorgeously. After that, when we landed, we took the airport bus. When I saw it, I couldn't even believe that the bus could be driven in both the directions. I saw the steerings at the back and the front end of it. And it was the first time that I saw a bus which could be driven at both ends without turning it. I was completely astonished. My first plane. My first airport. A whole lot of strange new people. We took another flight from Hong Kong to the Philippines. I was just looking at the buses, airports and the people. The second plane was bigger than the earlier one, and it was a more enjoyable experience. This plane was more spacious. When I reached my seat and sat down, I was surprised, because now there was television in front of the seat. I thought that, 'I am the luckiest one, the person who has a television before his seat. Thank you God.' Then I looked around and discovered, each and every seat I could see had a television screen. I re-considered, 'Okay...I wasn't the only person, who is lucky to have a television before the seat.' After that I kept looking out through the window and I could see some double-decker planes. It was one of the most surprising experiences of my life.

As the plane took off, I could see drifting clouds all around. My thoughts too swirled around. My life was changing swiftly. From now on, I knew, each and every thing would be really very opposite of my past life. You want to know what happened. Why was I on that plane? How did I get to be flying out of Kathmandu in Nepal to the Philippines? I was an abandoned street child. What had happened to me after that? I was on cloud nine literally. I was flying to a really unique and the historical movement called the Global March Against Child Labour. This was the march of hope, designed to touch every nook and corner of the globe to sensitize governments, law makers, corporates and common people on child labour.

The Global March Against Child Labour is a worldwide conglomeration of trade unions, teachers and civil society organisations that work together towards the shared development goals of eliminating and preventing all forms of child labour and ensuring access to all children to free, meaningful and good quality public education. It mobilises and supports its constituents to contribute to local, national, regional and global *efforts and supports a range of international instruments relating to the protection and promotion of children's rights and engages with the United Nations, international and inter-governmental agencies on the same.*

The first Global March was unique in that, it was a march not just of activists, it was a survivors' march. Children who had been child labourers and victims of social discrimination were the actual heroes of the march. It was an inclusive movement where the illiterate and unprivileged children were determined to teach and enlighten the educated, the elite and governments worldwide about the importance of education for all children, rich or poor, the homeless and the abandoned, the affluent and the privileged. It was a first of its kind effort to show the world the true picture of child abuse and exploitation, through the eyes of the very children who have suffered as well, to make others feel their pain and sorrow.

The child marchers were communicating a simple but powerful message — that if the future of millions of children in this world is so dark, how could we expect a bright future for humankind? Children from all the continents were participating in this movement called the Global March, with a hope to bring about a new kind of revolution. I was one of them and just on the way to our destination Manila, where the first leg of the Global March was to be flagged off from. I was overwhelmed by this incredible opportunity.

My chaperon tapped my shoulder and said, 'It's dinner time.'

As I turned my head, I could see beautiful air hostesses and smart stewards coming up the aisle to serve food to me, rolling forward their trolleys. I just couldn't believe that this was happening to me. The food was so delicious. I had never had food like this before. I thought it was magic, I wondered if these pretty angels had cooked it. It was the best food that I had ever had in my life. After having dinner, I closed my eyes and started to think about the Global March because I was chosen as one of the core marchers to represent millions of other children who weren't on that airplane. It was the defining moment of my life.

The pain which Global March was about to share with the world, was with the hope of bringing new light to the lives of many similar other children. I was glad that I was chosen as one of the core marchers to give voice to the most vulnerable in this world. I felt blessed that I had got a worldwide platform to argue the case for opportunities for destitute children so that their dream for parity in education and access could become a reality, because I had gone through the same pain and struggle. Yet, as I slunk down deep in my seat, dozing, it was strange to think that just a few years ago, my life was completely different from the one in an airplane, traveling to distant lands. My past came back to me like a picture post-card.

ഇൗരുൗരു

Riches To Rags

Every day when the sun rose, I darted towards those containers of garbage which were full of litter, crap, rotten and decayed food which stank badly. In spite of that, I flipped trash around and searched for my life in it. I just kept rummaging in trash for hours and hours, but I never found my life in these garbage cans and rotten food. I filled my stomach and stayed alive.

How vastly different was my life; every normal child slung a backpack and moved towards school. To get educated and be something in life. But my schedule was very different from everyone else. I did not have a haversack or satchel. Instead, I had a sack at my back filled with tin cans, plastics, packets and scrap, throwaways and smelly crap. The rucksacks of school children spread the fragrances of books, and the light of knowledge, my sack smelled of litter. Because our sacks were different, our destinies and destinations were different. But each and every piece of paper which I collected from the dust bins, gave me the knowledge to survive in this world and emerge as hope for tomorrow's dawn. They decided my real destination because I need to give some light to this world.

It was after the brawl with knives with the junkies that I had decided, I would no longer pick pockets. Early in the morning, one of my friends gave me a huge sack. I was so surprised. The sack was bigger than I was. I said to him, 'Hey! Buddy. We can sleep in it at night, it is pretty good and large... Isn't it?' He laughed and replied, 'Yeah! And come on...let's have a cup of tea and we'll go to work.' We both just walked up to the tea stall and each had a cup of tea and buns. After that, the whole day we were searching for rags, scraps, tips of containers, certain kinds of plastic, iron, aluminum articles. Entire day, we searched and collected such bits and pieces articles. We stuffed these in our sacks. And in the evening, we took these to a place where people bought such litter. They gave us money for what we brought. It was regular work. We earned honestly. It was a litter plant where they used to send litter for recycling. We used to get different amounts of money for different items. For plastic articles, we used to get Rs 16 per kilogram, Rs 60 for copper, Rs 6 for iron and Rs 20 for aluminum. Every day, I used to do the same work and the work was very hard and the money was too little. Every day I had to go to different dump sites to search out saleable material. It was too stinky and dirty work. So, soon, I was totally fed up. I then began to steal articles like copper, aluminum utensils from different houses. I would smash these up very roughly and I used to sell these to the litter plant.

I used to feel very bad because every day, I had to start my day with the dirty litter yards, which stank and were very difficult to tolerate. But what could I do? I had to do ragpicker's work because there wasn't any option to survive in the street in any other somewhat honest way. I used to feel alone while working. My friends and I did different things in different locations. We met only at night and we indulged in a great deal of vandalism.

It was one such winter night. Our gang was ambling down the middle of the road and some of our friends were humming songs. The road was completely deserted. We couldn't hear anything except our own voices and the words of the songs my friends were singing. We could just see the street lights which illuminated the lonely roads, and not a single vehicle moved around. As I looked around, I could see the houses that had lights already turned off. Sometimes we could hear barking of stray dogs but the city seemed to be dead and we were the only ones, a gang of boys, alive and wandering down an entombed empire; we were the kings of the road. The roads were ours, there wasn't anyone anywhere to stop us from doing anything; we could go where we wanted to, do just what we wanted to. On the spur of the moment Lama said, 'Hey man, there should be something rocking today, what do you think?'

In the meanwhile, I had just found a tin can and had started to kick it, trying to send it flying as far as I could. All of a sudden, Kumar said, 'Let's frigging play soccer.' He took the tin can, then passed it to Lama. As he stopped the can, Lama said, 'He said let's frigging play! Come and get it.' Everyone then scrambled around, trying to snatch the can from each other. Gradually we got tired and started to sigh restlessly. We sat down for a while. Then just kept strolling. As we were ambling down the road, I saw the car. It was parked near a big building. I told Lama, 'Hey, Lama! I want to drive a car.'

Lama was startled and said, 'You blo... Basu. You seem to be completely out of your mind. Are you alright? We don't have a car to drive. So from where are you going to drive?' I grinned and replied, 'You dumb p...! Can't you see the car right in front? It's parked in front of that building.' Suddenly, Kumar spoke up and said, 'Hey! Don't blo... say that. We may get caught and I don't freaking want to commit suicide. So just keep walking and forget about it.' I provoked them and said, 'You scumbags. You seem to be complete losers and don't possess any nerve anymore. Go! Freaking piss offs! Get out of my sight.' I spoke like I was a big dad, a gang leader. I was the youngest of them all.

Lama was furious and replied in a harsh voice, 'Okay you perky never-going-to-listen-to-anyone. Always trying to act a tough guy, yeah? You think you got more guts than any of us alright? Let's go and drive that blo… car. I'm not a fri…loser! You heard me. I'm freaking not a loser! And don't blo…try to call me that again.' Everyone started to chuckle at him and I smiled and said, 'Okay, I heard that you are not a loser; so what are we waiting for? Let's go!'

As we reached the car, Kumar said, 'Hey, how the heck are we going to open it? Its blo…locked.' When I heard this, I picked up a big stone and smashed the car window. Lama said, 'Holy shit! What the heck are you trying to do man! We are seriously scre…d up man!' I replied in haste, 'Shut up! And push the car as soon as possible, otherwise we'll seriously get nicked.' Kumar and I got into the car and tried to drive it. The rest of the gang began to push the car. So, there we were, taking turns at steering the big car and the others were pushing the car. Suddenly a cop appeared behind us and shouted at us, 'Wait! You sons of b…. I'm not going to leave you.' As we saw the policeman running toward us, we just jumped out of the car and all of us took to our heels in full speed. We were lucky that night, the police could not catch us, otherwise it would have meant serious jail time for us.

After running some miles, I halted and took a deep breath and started to pant rapidly. Others too stopped and panted like dogs. Lama said, 'Thank God, we didn't get caught!' I grinned and said, 'Well it was really fun, though.' Kumar also supported me and said, 'Yes boy. It was really fun and that nasty cop couldn't even catch us.' Then he chuckled. I told Lama, 'Hey! Lama, I think we should do this things often, yeah!' Lama looked at me and said, 'Of course, brother. I would really love to do this again. Please be ready to shove the cop's cudgel up your ass.' I laughed at him and said, 'Sure. be my guest. C'mon chums, don't worry. That day will not come soon.' I gestured at him, as if I were shooting him, with my two fingers and winked at him. So, for some time after that, trying to drive away parked cars became our regular form of entertainment.

Next morning, my friends made a plan to go to the movies. They were spruced up nicely and ready for the film but no one had told me about their plans. As I saw them, I asked them, 'Hey! For what are these smart soldiers ready? Anyway, you guys are looking like a bunch of thieves.' Then I grinned. Lama was annoyed. He said, 'You dumb pr….. We are looking like thieves to you, yeah?' I smiled and said, 'No doubt, buddy.' Kumar then said, 'Hey! Basu. We are going to the movies. Lama said that you cannot go with us because you stink badly and have no clean clothes.' I was furious and I asked, 'I am what?' Lama replied, 'You look so nasty. And for going to the movies, you need some nice clothes and have to smell nice.' I was mad, and said, 'You d…ags, trying to go to the movies without me? That blo… sucks. You bug…s. You are ready to share my bloody stolen money and ready to have fun together but now that you know that I don't have money today, and no bloody good clothes, so you are going without me?'

Kumar felt sorry. So he put his right hand on my shoulder and said, 'C'mon Basu. Don't take it seriously.' I was so enraged, I replied dryly, 'You pinky, don't bloody try to make excuses. You better bugger off from here.' As I said this, I turned around and walked on. May be, they felt they had wronged me and realised their mistake. They hurried after me and said, 'Hey! Basu. C'mon man. We are friends and we were just kidding. We came to call you too.' I again turned to them and said, 'Don't you idiots dare lie now.' Lama said, 'I'm sorry now. Let's go and find some neat clothes for you. C'mon please…' Finally I agreed to go along with them, but when they calculated the money they had, there wasn't enough for my new clothes. Kumar said, 'Oh Shit! We don't have money to buy the clothes.' I replied, 'Hey! Kumar. Don't worry about the money.' Lama said, 'Oh! It means you got some, yeah?' I smiled.

Just smiled and said, 'No. But I got an idea.' Kumar got scared and said, 'No! Not freaking again! You dork. You always play with bloody life and one day, we are going to get killed by your schemes and adventures.'

Lama said, 'This bugger's clothes are so dirty and you can probably be sure there's is lice in it. And we don't have even a single penny for new clothes. So tell me Genius, what's your idea?' I smiled and pointed to the terrace of a two-storey house near by, where nice and damp clothes were dangling on the rope, hung out to be dried. Lama said, 'Oh heck!' I grinned and provoked them, 'You guys got nerves yeah?' Kumar asked, 'What are you really planning to do?' I asked Lama, 'Are you ready brother?' He gave me a really weird look and said, 'Let's do it!' Kumar again asked, 'Would somebody tell me what we are really going to do?' I chuckled and said, 'I'm thinking of stealing those clothes on the terrace.' Kumar was scared and shouted, 'No way! No, don't do that.' I grinned and said, 'You are such a coward.' Then I ran towards the house. Behind me, I heard Kumar's voice saying, 'Holy shit! We are dead now.'

I gave the thumbs up signal to Lama and then climbed up on the roof through the rainwater pipes and threw all the clothes down from the rope hastily. But in my hurry, I unfortunately broke a TV antenna, while I was pulling a jacket down. Suddenly, one old man came to the roof. Guess, he had been watching television but I broke the aerial, so he had come up to investigate why he had lost connection. He saw me stealing the clothes. First he was too shocked to figure out what was really going on. He stared at me, his eyes popping out. I too was immobilised momentarily, still clutching the jacket. Suddenly he came to life and began screaming, 'Thief! Thief ! Hey! You wait... I'll kill you bastard, you just wait....' He picked up a long iron rod and came charging at me and said, 'You stupid kid, what did you think? Nobody at home? Now run if you can... Hi! Hi! Hi!' He laughed and said, 'Where will you run...? There is no way to go... are you going to jump off from here hmn...?'

I was terrified. I thought I was dead. At the moment, I couldn't think of anything. I just jumped off the roof in a panic.

Fortunately, there was a heap of sand on the ground. So I just sprained my legs. As I brushed myself and stood up, I couldn't believe that I was still alive. It was a suicidal flight. I couldn't understand that I was really alive. I was totally numb. My friends ran to me and picked me up. We then ran away from there. After that, we went to the public bathroom, had a bath. Then we changed clothes and went to the doctor. One of my friends paid the doctor's fee. Then he said, 'Come on... let's go to a restaurant and have something to eat. I am very hungry now.' Lama replied, 'It means, we will not be able to go for the movie, since there is less money left now as I paid the doctor.'

I was limping because I had pain. One of my friends suddenly spoke up and admired me, 'Howdy champion? You were too great, And lucky as well. You jumped off from the

two-storey building. I thought you were dead. Very good
Basu. You really got guts! Actually, in this world there are
very few lucky people and luck is on your side nowadays.
So keep it on.' He patted my back. I was really calm. I had
confronted death just a few moments ago. I had to prove
myself tough. I quickly replied: 'You know what? My life
is not to be eliminated like that. In fact, I have to do lots
of great things in my life. I can tell you that one day, you
all will be proud of me. May be, we will not meet or be
together. But I do have very big ambitions. This vicious
street is not meant for me Raju. My goal is very different
from this bloody street.'

Ram Kumar, yet another friend, laughed and spoke in a
sarcastic manner, 'Aye, yeah...You will surely do something
in your life. Perhaps, when you grow up, you will wipe your
doo-doo and other people's as well. That's what you will do in
your life. Well... ambition of wiping other people's bottoms
also not bad... hi! hi! Hi!' He continued to laugh and slowly,
all the others began to smirk, mocking and grinning at me.
A friend, who was quite mature and known as Ajay, pointed
to another friend and said, 'You know....? Our friend is a
homo and he is richer than all of us. But as you see, his ass
is getting wider and wider. I think you will be very rich if
you follow him.'

The boy who was named, he chuckled along with
everyone else. Then he said, 'Don't feel bad. Look at me.

This is real life and we have to enjoy it. I can't be rich because it is my fate to be a street boy. Even God wants this. We don't know where we took birth. Where our parents are. They threw us to the streets to enjoy this life, do you get that? But you bug...! You are really different. You talk extraordinary things in life. It's like a dream world where you live my friend. C'mon...! Come to real life. Get out of the dreaming world and face reality which is this street. Let's enjoy. Who knows if we will be alive tomorrow or not.' I put my hand on his shoulder and said, 'I am going to change my life. That's a promise to you all pessimists. And that is a challenge for my fate and destiny.' They all spoke up at once when I replied. 'Okay...okay.' Raju smiled and said, 'Dreaming rich is okay, but what about today's food? I'm hungry.' Everybody laughed.

ဢၵ‌ဢၵ

A Servant Boy

*W*hen a deadly storm comes, and the blizzard pushes you and rain batters you, you are likely to run to a shelter. People get shelter inside their homes when the outside element are rough. Many like me are not lucky to run to any shelter. They are homeless. They live on the streets and take shelter on the streets. I at least found other people's homes to take shelter in. This was a life I had chosen for a while. I was a little different from others. When people slept, I used to wake up and clean mosaic floors, tried hard to see my own future in the reflections on these polished floors. When people had breakfast, I used to wash dishes on empty stomach. When people went to office, I used to go to see my owner's children to the school bus, hanging their water bottles and backpacks on my shoulder. When other children got love at home, I used to get beaten by my owner. So, *when people were normal, I used to be abnormal and gradually I accepted the fact that, having an abnormal life was the normal thing for me. At the same time I realized that having a home is a beautiful thing, because you feel like a king. You don't feel, you are a born slave. History is witness, working as a slave is not easy.*

Gadding around with empty pockets in the maze of the streets, I just kept walking and walking. It was like a sort of madness. I didn't stop walking. I just put one step ahead of another. Like I didn't know how to stop it. After five hours of crazy ambling along through the streets, I was suddenly jostled by a person. It was funny that I fell down and the person who bumped into me apologised quickly, and helped me to stand up. He said, 'Sorry kid, are you okay?' I didn't reply. It was strange for me, I was lost somewhere. It was sort of an unconscious moment. I could hear the hustle and bustle of the street and people were busy as bees. Some explored around to buy something. The shops had just opened and shopkeepers were shouting, trying hard to sell their stuff. I had walked along in a dream, unknown to myself.

Suddenly I saw a fruit stall and became aware that I was starving. So I went near the shop, which was crowded, As I put my hand in my pocket, I realised there wasn't a single paisa left in it. But I was desperately hungry and wanted something to eat, it was as if my intestines within were writhing and screaming, 'How to get an apple to quench the fire of hunger, which is burning inside?' This is when I began scheming, 'If I ask the shopkeeper for the apple, he will not give me. So it is better to steal it.' A lot of people were buying fruit. They looked fresh and lovely. I was smacking my lips but the problem was, how to get it? I mingled in the crowd. People were jostling each other, so I also bumped into a few of them, and pretended, as if I was also trying to buy fruit. All the time I kept watch that the shopkeeper should not notice me. I moved my hand towards an apple, but then I flinched. I felt the shopkeeper was looking at me. But he wasn't. His attention was elsewhere. After a while, one woman looked at me. But soon she was busy choosing fruits. Eventually, I managed to grab an apple and ran away, and didn't look back.

I found a pavement which was near the tea shop we frequented. So I sat down and started to bite into my apple. It was then that one man came near to me and asked me, 'Hi! Are you alone?'

I was startled. I couldn't figure out, why he was asking me that? He seemed to be nice and some tycoon sort of a guy with a briefcase in his hand. I thought this person appeared to be benevolent. I answered him glumly, 'Sir, I am an orphan. I pass my time here on the road. This apple which I'm eating is stolen. I don't have a single penny, nor a job.' The answer was pointless because he had just asked me how was I? I had tried to be smart. I thought I could get some help from him. He admired me for speaking the truth and offered me a job. 'You are a smart and bold guy. I like it. So, would you like to work in a house?' I was surprised at the way he offered me the job! I did not want the chance to go away, so I answered him, 'Yes, Sir. I really want to work. I hope it will be in your house, isn't it?'

He answered, 'No... not in my house. But it is bigger than my house. I do have a friend and his wife wanting a boy for help in their house.' I replied, 'Okay. I'm ready. But how much will they provide me as a monthly salary?' He smiled and said, 'you little chap. You are very sharp. One day, you will be the king of this world.' Then he continued, 'Around three or four hundred per month. Plus you will get food daily, clothes and accommodation. Is it enough for you?' I was very happy and started to talk to myself and told myself, 'this day seems quite a lucky day...Thank God.' That man then asked me abruptly, 'Hey, what happened? What are you thinking?' He poked me. I replied, 'Nothing, Sir.'

I began walking along with this stranger. 'So, where do we go now?' We went to the telephone booth where he made a call. After that he said, 'Okay, let's's go.' I then asked him for food. 'Sir, since yesterday I am dying of starvation. Will you give me some food?' He grinned and said, 'Hey, not to worry. Let's go to the hotel and have something. Even I'm hungry.' I was very happy to be with this man, he seemed to be a jolly good person. We went to a nice hotel and he asked me, 'What would you like to have?' I asked him to give me any cheap stuff to eat and let me quench my hunger. He asked me, 'Do you eat chicken?' I heard it and I said, 'Of course, Sir. I love it actually. I didn't tell you because I thought it would be very expensive for you and you are a nice person. So, I didn't want to make you spend a lot of money.'

He again looked at me with startled eyes and said, 'You are a very nice kid. At such a tiny age, you have a nice mind. It's good.' He ordered chicken for me and he had noodles and one piece of chicken. After having lunch, the waiter came and gave him a bill. The man took out money from his purse and put it on the bill pad. After that, the waiter came back with some change. It was around fifty rupees. The man got up and said, 'keep the change' to the waiter. The waiter smiled and said, 'Thank you, Sir.' I suddenly snatched the change from the waiter's hand and said, 'You bugger. What did you think? I'll give you the money? Come on. Don't ever try to fool anyone, you got me?' The waiter gazed at me angrily and then we got out of that hotel.

My benefactor took me towards the car parking and said, 'Okay, get in.' I was surprised. For the first time somebody had told me, 'Get into the car.' Not bad. Thank God. When I entered the car, I looked around and then suddenly, I missed my Pop because I knew that the first car I sat in was my father's car. Whenever my Pop used to be free, he used to go for long drives along with me, and he would talk about my Mom and cry sometimes. This was strange. This man's car was black and coincidently, like my Pop's car. I became very serious and started to explore the car. The man asked me what happened. I remained quiet and said nothing for a while. Then suddenly I told him, 'I miss my Pop.' He didn't understand and asked me, 'What do you mean by Pop?' I replied, 'I called my father Pop since I started to speak, and he used to say the first word I spoke was Pop.' He scoffed and said, 'It's very strange. I have heard that the first word a child speaks is Mom. But in your case it is a little different.'

He asked me, 'Where is your Pop?' I replied, he is dead. 'He was dead when I was four.' The man nodded, then he asked me, 'So, how old are you now?' I speculated and replied, 'around seven.' It was then my turn to ask questions. I asked him, 'How old is your car? Did you buy it second hand?' He said, 'No... no, it is one year old and I bought it first hand which is brand new.' I said, 'I am asking because this car might be older than I am.' He asked me again, 'Do you remember the place where your dad and you lived?' I immediately said, 'Yes. Kathmandu.' He grinned and said, 'No. The proper place. This is also Kathmandu and where you are going to work is also Kathmandu. It is a small city but not that small to find your house easily.' I knew that I had forgotten the name of the place where my home had been. So I remained quiet. I asked him one more question. 'Do you have kids?' He seemed happy to remember them.

'They are small yet, your age.' I again asked him, 'Do you love them?' He replied sternly, 'More than my life.'

During these conversations, we had reached our destination, his friend's house. He honked at the gate. I saw through the car window, it was an immense house. The watchman opened the gate and said, 'Good afternoon, Sir.' I was surprised again and he halted the car in the parking. Then he said, 'So, little boy. This is the place and it was nice meeting you. Let's go upstairs and let me introduce you to everyone.' I was surprised to see the place. And when we finally reached upstairs, I was really startled to see the huge rooms and the people. He introduced me to the mistress and master of the house. They all looked at me and said, 'Well...this lad is quite smart. Anyway, where are you from?' I replied very innocently, 'I'm from nowhere because I forgot the place my home was in Madam. And unfortunately, I'm a stray child.' She was speechless for a while. 'Okay.' Then she went to the kitchen and brewed tea and brought it in glittering cups and she put it on the table and asked me, 'Do you want to have it too?' I replied, 'Yes.' She handed me a cup of tea and gave another to the man who had brought me here. She took one cup of tea for herself.

After finishing the tea, the man said, 'Okay then. I got to go now, because I am getting a bit late. I have to go to school to bring my children home. Actually my wife had to go shopping and she has passed on the job to me. So I really have to go.' Then the mistress of the house replied, 'Okay then… please keep coming home sometimes.' He smiled and said, 'Sure.' Then he glared at me and said, 'So, young man. It was nice to have had a very good conversation with you. Hope to see you in the future. Okay, bye.' I felt uneasy because I knew him and we had mingled with each other like good friends. After his departure, I was sitting on the sofa. Then suddenly, I heard the mistress's voice. When I swung my head towards her, she asked me to come along with her and she said, 'See, I have to be clear about each and every thing which you have to do in this home. So, let me tell you this house is very big and you have to sweep and mop each and every corner of this house. It should be absolutely clean, alright?' I was astonished. The house was immense. I was a small child. It would take me hours to clean this house. Suddenly she asked, 'What happened?'

I answered, 'Nothing.' She was eager to explain to me all the household chores. At the same time, she said, 'You must keep one thing in your mind whenever guests come here, that you should address me as a "Madam". So start from today.' Hearing her, a thought came to my mind, 'Why couldn't she have been a little friendly with me?' She asked me, 'What are you thinking?' I replied to her quickly, 'I'm a little worried about cleaning the whole house. It's really big and it will take lots of time to finish.' She was restless. She didn't care about how small I was and said,

'Yes. There is a woman who comes early in the morning but she is a little expensive and it is very unsafe to let her clean the whole house because there has been certain cases of stealing. So, tomorrow onwards, I'm going to tell her to quit the job and pay her for whatever time she gave for our house. So, from now on, you are going to handle this whole house, young boy.' I felt nervous. She then added to my list of responsibilities, saying, 'You don't forget to finish your sweeping and moping before 6 o'clock in the morning because after that, you have to go to the school-bus stand, along with Sama, to escort her.'

Sama was her pampered daughter. That night, when everyone returned home, I was startled to see that there were six members in the house. Master and mistress, their two children who were a daughter and son, and then finally, the kids' grandparents. They all sat together at the dining table and I brought the meal from the kitchen to the dining table and served them. Everyone was very happy to see the new little servant. They asked me my name while I was serving them.

They were having dinner and I was just standing by the side of the dining table, according to my mistress' command and I was doing those things my mistress told me to do. Sometimes, master would call me and tell me to serve him the pulses. I would run quickly as they called me. After finishing their dinner, every one got up from the table and

I collected all the plates and took them to the kitchen. After that I stayed at the wash basin, separating plate and the scrap. Suddenly, I heard my mistress' voice, 'Hey! Don't forget to clean all the utensils and don't break any of them, you get me?' I said, 'Don't worry, Madam; I will not let you down.' I cleaned all the utensils till 9 o'clock. All the members of the house were watching television. After washing all the utensils, I went to the drawing room and sat there. Then, finally, my mistress asked, 'Have you eaten anything?' I replied, 'No.'

She called me to the kitchen and put food in a plate and asked me to eat it. I was starved and I sat on the floor and started to eat it very quickly. She then said, 'See. Tomorrow onwards, I will not give you food after finishing our dinner. You can eat the remaining food, okay?' I replied in a low voice, 'Sure, Madam.' She left the kitchen and again came back and said, 'and another thing. After cleaning up everything, you can sleep in the drawing room, okay?' I replied to her very obediently, 'Okay.' It was around 10 o'clock at night, when everyone had gone to bed that I put off the lights and lay down in the drawing room hall.

Next morning, very early, the mistress came to the drawing room and started to shake me awake. I was very sleepy and I asked her in sleep, 'What happened?' She was annoyed. 'What happened? You need to get up right now and start to do the housework...come on...get up now.' I got up and started to rub my eyes, then she spoke, 'From tomorrow onwards, you have to get up yourself. Nobody will come to wake you up, alright? And the second thing, this is the alarm clock and the time is already set on it. You need to press this button before going to sleep and to put the alarm on and press it again to put off the alarm when you get up, okay?'

In a gruff voice, I said, 'Alright, Madam.' I walked towards the bathroom and picked up the bucket and turned on the tap, then started to fill it. While the water was filling, I searched for the mop and then began to swab the floors, from the top to the ground floor. It took me nearly two hours to do this. After that, mistress' beautiful princess got up and started to get ready for school. Suddenly, the milkman arrived and mistress asked me to bring the milk in. I walked downstairs and reached the gate. The milkman asked me, 'Are you the new servant of this house?' I replied with a smile, 'Yes, old man.' I gave him the jug. He started to pour the milk in it and said, 'You don't seem to be a servant.' I asked him, 'Why?' He smiled. 'You are fair and clean. You are like a member of the house.' I smiled and replied, 'I'm not that lucky, old man.'

All of a sudden, the watchman said, 'Hey! Mistress is calling you.' I smiled and asked him, 'How do you know that mistress is calling me? Do you think I am a mug or what?' The watchman replied gruffly, 'You stupid stub. She called me on the phone, you got that?' I was startled, but continued asking, 'Well… yes… but I cannot understand, how she can call you at the gate?' The watchman replied dryly, 'The phones are extended all over the house plus to this gate too… you got that idiot?' I said nothing more except, 'Hum…' Then he said, 'That's good. Now go upstairs and follow the command of the mistress.' I lifted the milk jug and started to climb the stairs. When I reached the top floor, I walked into the kitchen and kept the milk jug on the marble table top. Mistress was running here and there and was very busy, making breakfast for her children. She packed this into the tiffin boxes and stuffed the boxes into the school bags. Then she told me to pick up both the bags and she told me to go downstairs and wait at the gate. I hung both the bags on my back and started to trudge down the stairs again. When I reached the gate, I leaned against the wall and waited. I so very much wanted to go to school, just like all the other children.

I saw the two neat and well-dressed children approaching me with the mistress. When they reached the gate, mistress told me to go with them up to the bus stand, carrying their school bags. She told me, 'Don't hang around. Just directly come back home.' I nodded and got out of the gate. I was trudging along with them. The children were as old as I was. The girl was called Sama. She asked me my name once more, 'What's your name?' I told her my name but she did not like it. I smiled and said, 'It doesn't matter. Whatever you want to call me, just call me.' She grinned and stretched her hand toward me. 'You are so sweet, would you be our friend?' I answered her with a smile, 'Sure!' I extended my hand towards the brother and sister. But the school bag suddenly fell down and I apologised, 'I'm sorry, it's my fault.' Sama quickly bend forward and lifted the bag up and asked me to carry only one bag, that of her brother. I did not want her to take her bag, but she said, 'You are our friend right? So it doesn't matter…And even then, it is too heavy for you. And don't worry about your mistress, we won't tell Mom, okay?'

I was so happy that I had found some friends, who were very nice. We were walking constantly. She asked me about my family. 'Well…where are your Mom and Dad?' I did not know what to tell her but my heart said, I shouldn't lie to anyone. So I said, 'My dad and my mom, they are very far from me, and especially my dad. He is with God.' She was surprised and asked me, 'You mean, your dad is dead?' I said, 'That's right. But he can see me every time, everywhere, wherever I am. You want to see my dad?' She said, 'Yes, but how?'

'At night, I always see the sky. I like it and I have heard that if somebody dies, they become stars. So, my dad is also in the sky.'

She said, 'We will see tonight alright?' I was so glad to get such a nice friend here and it was a nice start to the day for me. In the meanwhile, we had reached the bus stand. There were other children, I had begun to just look at each one of them. All of a sudden, Sama said, 'Have you ever been to school?' It was a pretty strange question for me. I was quiet for a while and then replied, 'I have never been to school.' She said, 'Okay....' Then one of her friends arrived and wished her, 'Hi! Good morning... so how are you?' Sama replied, 'Fine.' The friend then looked at me and asked her, 'Who is he?' Sama said, 'He is our new friend.' The friend then wished me good morning! In English. I replied, 'Good morning!' And I asked her, 'How are you?' Her friend replied, 'I'm good and you?' I answered her, 'I'm okay.' Sama was looking at me and she asked me in a surprised manner, 'How do you know English?' I said, I don't know but I can understand it very well. 'But can't speak it nicely.' Sama then said, 'You know, for English, we have to study a lot. But you can speak it without studying anything. Amazing!'

The school bus came and honked. I gave Sama's brother his bag and then all the children boarded the bus. It started to move away, when the children began to wave to me, still standing at the bus stop. 'Bye.' I also waved my hand back at them. Then, slowly, I walked back to the bungalow. Mistress called me and asked me, 'Why are you so late?' I didn't have any answer. But I tried to explain to her as much as possible, 'I'm coming directly home Madam.' she warned me again, not to tarry at the bus stand. I was very scared by her style of conversation. She called me into the kitchen and taught me how to prepare tea. I must say, it was the second time that I was learning to brew tea because I knew how to brew tea. She asked me, 'do you know how to prepare food?' I said, 'No Ma'am. I… really don't know how to prepare food but I can learn quickly, if you teach me.' She said, no it was okay, but from her expression I understood that she was not exactly interested in me cooking the food. Instead, she again called me and asked me to go to the bathing room and wash all the clothes which were lying there.

As I entered the bathroom, I saw this huge pile of clothes lying in a heap, like a small pyramid, all for me to wash. Some were big and heavy, some of the garments were light. But, anyway, all of them had to be washed. And I began to wash them, one by one. Soon Madam followed me to the bathroom and told me, 'use the soap nicely. Don't waste it unnecessarily, you got that?' By that time, I was tired and my waist had started to ache. Madam picked up one garment, rubbed soap on it, then beat it on the floor, showing me how to do it. 'Have you got it… how to wash clothes?' 'Yes Ma'am I got you very well…and it is so kind of you to teach me how to wash clothes.' I went on washing clothes. I had lost count of time. Mistress then came to the bathing room and asked me, 'How long will you take to wash these few garments? You are sitting here since morning. But you haven't completed it yet.' I was very hungry and irritated by mistress' nagging. My waist was also paining.

Suddenly she asked me, 'Are you hungry?' I said, 'Yes Ma'am. I'm starving.' She then called me to the kitchen and gave me some rice and pulse to eat. I sat on the floor near the wash basin, and then started to stuff the food into my mouth very quickly. I felt very nice, as if I had poured water on a mad fire, to extinguish it. After that my mistress commanded me, 'Hey! Now listen very carefully. After you have finished your lunch. Wash all the utensils, whatever has been used and clean the kitchen very well. Then you go and do your washing stuff and remember, don't take a lot of time to wash the clothes, because you have to do other work too. You got that?' I just bobbed my head but didn't utter even a single word. My cruel mistress had slept the whole day and I was doing all the work in the house. I was so angry, I could have gladly strangled her, little that I was.

But one thing I understood very well that day. Doing household chores was not easy. I wouldn't get even a single minute to relax. After cleaning the kitchen and dishes, I returned to the bathroom and to the pile of clothes. I had no choice. Those clothes really sucked. So I started to stamp and jump on them, rinsing them with clean water. Squeezing and wringing the clothes was really tough, because it shook every bone in my body. Finally, I was ready to hang them on wires to get dry, but unfortunately, it was already evening, the sun was setting. I was just lifting the bucket of clothes when mistress arrived and asked, 'Where are you going?' I said, 'I'm going to put these clothes to dry.' She was angry and blamed me, 'Because of your procrastination, we missed the sunny day and now the sun is set. The clothes would have dried if you had done them earlier.' I bowed my head and listened. 'Anyway, now go and put these attires to dry and don't forget to put the clips on them, you got me?' I quickly replied, 'Yes Ma'am.' I lifted the bucket of clothes and walked upstairs to the roof.

When I reached the roof, I saw the mistress' two kids, who were playing. They saw me too and asked me, 'Hey! How are you?' I replied, 'Okay… but totally bushed.' They wanted to know why? I told them about all the work I had done the whole long day. They were children and they understood me better than their cruel mother. They offered to help but I refused because I was afraid of the mistress. Then I started to hang out the clothes on the wire. They did not listen to me and began to help me, also hanging out the clothes to dry. After finishing with the bucket of clothes, they asked me to play with them but I refused. I had yet another bucket of clothes to dry. I went down and brought up the other two buckets of washed clothes. I started to hang out clothes, when the two children came again to help me by fixing the clips on the spread out clothes. My new-found little friends helped me.

After completing the task of spreading out the clothes to

dry, Sama, asked me, 'Why do you do such a lot of work?' I quickly gave her the answer, 'Actually I'm a poor boy. I don't have any money to live, that's why.' She again asked me, 'How much money will my Mom give you after a month?' I said, 'Around three hundreds rupees a month.' She was very surprised. 'You know, my Mom gives me daily two hundreds rupees for my canteen stuff, when I go to school. You work very hard, you should get a lot of money for it.' I told her, 'It is luck. There are a lot of unbalanced things which make for the balance in this world. For instance, you and me.' She was totally puzzled by what I said. 'Well. I really could not get what you meant. But I can say one thing. You speak like my teacher.' I sniggered at her. She said, 'Don't snigger. I really mean it.' Suddenly, I heard the voice of my mistress. She was calling me, and asking me to come down to the kitchen to help her cook dinner.

I was about to go down, when Sama asked me, 'Do you know how to ride a bicycle?' I said, 'Of course.' She asked me, 'Will you teach me to ride?' I told her in a serious manner, 'Well... it will be very difficult right now, because your mom is calling me. Perhaps, the next time?' She smiled and caught my hand and said, 'Come with me.' She took me to her mom and asked her, 'Mom, he knows how to ride the bicycle, and I want to learn it. Ask him to teach me.' Mistress looked at me and asked me, 'You know how to ride a bicycle?' I said, 'Yes, Ma'am.' Then she said, 'Okay, then you go and teach her to ride the bicycle for twenty minutes. And then you come directly to the kitchen to help me, alright? And remember, don't let her fall.' I quickly said, 'Sure Ma'am.' Then we ran downstairs. Sama took the bicycle and asked me to teach her. I asked her to sit on the seat of the bicycle and told her I would hold her. She sat on the seat and I held the bicycle and started to push it. I was also pretty happy, because after the day-long work, at last this was a fun thing I was doing.

Again I heard the same annoying voice of my mistress. She was calling me upstairs to help her in the kitchen. I now told Sama, 'I got to go know, because your mom is calling me. Listen, if you want me to teach you to ride the bicycle, ask your mom to spare me for some time every day. That's the only way I can teach you to ride and I can at least get the chance to ride that bicycle too. She said, 'Okay.' Then I ran up the stairs to the kitchen, where mistress was preparing dinner. She asked me to cut the vegetables. I started to peel potatoes. I knew very well that after helping with preparing dinner, I would have to serve dinner to everyone, and then clean the dishes.

I did this tedious, back-breaking work for three long months very honestly. I never refused to do anything my mistress told me to do. It was very strange that despite being a very obedient boy, I had to one day face another 'worst day' in my life, a situation, where I was again almost at death's door. And for what? It is difficult for me to forget that Sunday. Even now, I am totally traumatised when I try to recall that Sunday.

My mistress and master, and most of the family had to go shopping because it was my mistress' birthday. The two children were left at home. All the adults in the house went out. Before leaving the house, my mistress didn't forget to tell me about all the work I had to finish by a certain time, before they returned. As usual, I bobbed my head very politely and agreed. She then called out to her two children and told them not to be mischievous in her absence. She growled at me, 'What are you listening to? Go and wash the coffee mugs and cauldrons.' So, as usual, first I went to mop the floor. After two hours of work, I went and mowed the lawn because it was my mistress' order. I had left the cleaning of the utensil for the last. After three hour of mowing the lawn, I went to the kitchen and started to wash some dishes. Unfortunately, I dropped a coffee mug on to the floor and it was shattered. The noise was loud. Suddenly, Sama came to the kitchen and asked me, 'Did you break something?' I was very scared. But I told her, 'I broke the coffee mug accidentally.' She saw the mug and screamed, 'Oh! No! It was the mug which was gifted by Dad to Mom today.'

I apologised for my mistake and she said, 'It's okay. Don't worry. So you are working since morning. Come now. Let's play carom board.' I left the utensils unclean and then walked along with her to play. I did not know what time it was and

I was very happy because I had won the game. Suddenly it had turned dark and my mistress had returned home. She at once realised, I had been playing with the children. 'You are playing with them. What about your tasks, which I had given you before we left the house? Have you finished all of them?' I was terrified. I had not done the dishes. And, I had broken her coffee mug. Yet, I answered her very confidently, 'Yes, Madam. I have done each and every job you assigned, Madam.' Then Mistress dropped her shopping on the sofa and headed to the kitchen, to make coffee for her husband. After a few minutes, she screamed and called me. I quickly darted to the kitchen and said, 'Yes, Madam.' She was so angry. 'Did you break my coffee mug?'

I trembled before her. 'Yes, Ma'am. Accidentally. It slipped from my hand while I was cleaning it. She suddenly hit me, slapped me hard. Again and again, she slapped me in blind fury. I was very frightened and started to cry. Then the master also arrived, and he too started to beat me. I cried louder and louder and the two of them continued to beat me harder. I began to bleed from my nose and mouth. All for just a small coffee mug. I couldn't understand how such a small object like a mug was more valuable than my life and blood. Then the two children also came into the kitchen. They kept pleading with their mother and father to stop beating me. But the two adults had turned into beasts. They did not listen to their own children. My lips were cut and blood was pouring down, on to the kitchen floor. After a few minutes, the two adults left me in the kitchen. I lay down on the floor, still crying and bleeding. In a little while, mistress and master came to the kitchen and asked me to get up. I couldn't get up, because I was badly hurt. Master was angry again because I couldn't obey his command. So, he kicked me hard in my stomach with his leather boot. It hurt terribly. I lost my voice for a minute. He again asked me to get up. But unfortunately, I simply couldn't. Master then kicked me hard again, this time on my back bone. I lay there on the floor like a crushed and trampled worm. I lay still, I could not move. Mistress then got scared, seeing me so completely still. She told her husband, 'Stop. He will die, because he is not even making any noise anymore.' They left me in the kitchen after that.

After an hour, mistress came to see me again. She called me and asked me to wipe the blood which had spilled on the ground, because she wanted to prepare dinner. Slowly, very slowly, I got up. I limped and got a mop and started to clean the floor of my spilled blood. It was really difficult to move my limbs. After that, I went to the terrace and sat quietly. I looked at the sky and asked God a simple question. 'Why God? Why just me? I work here for the whole day but nobody appreciates my work.' I was looking at the sky and thinking of the injustice, my eyes closed in fatigue.

I was sleeping on the terrace and the climate was not

warm. I had not eaten anything at all. The night was getting colder. All of a sudden, I heard her voice. 'Hey! Basu.' I slowly swung my head. It was Sama and her brother. They had brought dry fruits and a blanket for me. It was sweet of them. They said, 'Hey! It's around 11 pm. Quite late in the night. Have some dry fruits and sleep. Sorry we couldn't help you as much as we wanted to. But take care of yourself, we're going now.' As they were moving away, I called her, 'Hey! Sama, come here.' They both came and asked, 'What happened?' I asked them to bend towards me, and come closer. As they brought their heads closer, I kissed each of them on their cheek and said, 'Thank you very much. You have been very sweet. Your friendship is one thing I will not forget in my entire life.' I wrapped the blanket around me and began to chew on the dry fruits very slowly. I was in pain and it was very difficult to chew even the dry fruits.

I began to talk to God once more. 'Hey! Almighty. If I would have had brothers and sisters, would they have been this adorable and caring? So why didn't you give me brothers and sisters? Um….. Oh! You did right actually. When I am all alone, even then I am suffering a lot in this world. Had you given me a sister, what would she have been doing now? Anyway, thank you God and good night.'

જી(ર૪જી(ર

Breaking Free

In the morning, when I got up, it was almost time for Sama's school. I got up with a jerk but I forgot I was in pain even then. I scrambled downstairs and went to the drawing room and picked up both the school bags for the children. I went downstairs and waited for them. Mistress was looking at me, but didn't say anything.

I then went up to the gate and waited for them. Suddenly they came and we started to walk towards the bus stand. After a few steps, Sama and her brother, both took their respective bags and asked me to walk along with them. They carried their own school bags. Sama then said, 'Hey! Basu. We don't feel good that you are in so much pain. Anyway, take care of yourself.' I smiled. My lips were swollen. I still smiled and said, 'It's okay. I'm running away. I will drop you at the bus stand. In fact, you are my exit through this gate.' The children looked shocked. And sad. They were my friends. 'Where will you go?', they wanted to know. I replied, 'This world is very immense and I'm all alone since I was four years old. I have existed in this world so long. Let's see where my luck leads me.'

Sama fumbled in her pocket and took out three hundred rupees and said, 'Here take this. It's for you. It is my three days' pocket money. You keep it and use it for yourself.' Her brother also took out a hundred rupees he had in his pocket and gave me and said, 'this is from me. And I love you.' I was very happy to hear these words from this little boy. He was smaller than me, but he could understand what friendship meant. As we reached the bus stand, there were Sama's other friends, and many were my friends too. They were all very fond of me. After a short while, everyone got on to the school bus. Sama and her brother came to me and said, 'You take care, Basu. We love you a lot and we will not forget you. You are very sweet, and we have learnt lots of thing from you. Now I can speak like you too. Do you remember once you spoke like my teacher? Now everyone keep telling me that, "Sama you keep talking like a philosopher." And now, I know how to ride my bicycle. Thank you very much.'

That day I ran away. I was liberated from the life of servitude. But I felt that I had lost something very precious.

Yes, today I can say what I lost. I lost valuable things

like the love my owner's children had for an orphan boy.
The children were really innocent and pure hearted. They
were not contaminated by the so-called social norms. They
did not discriminate between the rich, poor, upper caste,
lower caste and so on. They only knew how to follow their
hearts. So I ran away and went back to the streets. I ambled
along aimlessly, just as I had done many many times before.
Suddenly, one very old pauper came before me and started
to beg and said, 'Son, God will bless you. You will be forever
happy in your life. Please give me something. I'm very
hungry.' I smiled at him and said, 'Come on... old man,
you don't have to flatter me such a lot to fill your tummy.
Actually, my life is not so good. And I don't think your
prayer will change anything in the rest of my life. Anyway,
you must be very hungry, isn't it?'

He gazed at me with bulging eyes, which were old and
sinking inwards, into his eye-holes. I told him, 'Don't worry,
old man. I was also a beggar earlier and I do understand
the burning and rumbling stomach. The fire of hunger
that people need to urgently extinguish. People have to
go through many thorny paths, which is sometimes very
painful, alright?' The beggar couldn't understand what
exactly I was saying to him, and he just kept looking at me.
I pulled him and said, 'You know, I have some money today.
And I am also feeling hungry. So, why don't we together have
something to eat today? Let's have something in the hotel

in front of us.' He was hesitant. I told him, 'Don't worry old man. You don't have to pay the bill.' He replied, 'No son. I'm not thinking of that. Actually, I know they will not allow me to get in.' I really understood what he meant and I said, 'Not to worry, old man. This world runs by money, if you have money you are allowed everywhere. If you don't, that means you are not allowed even to exist, you got me?'

When we were both about to enter the eatery's entrance, when the owner said, 'This dirty old man is not allowed in.' Even I did not look nice, because my face was still swollen from the previous night's assault, and I was not looking very different from the beggar. The old man smiled and said, 'Let it be son. I'll eat outside.' I sniggered and told the old pauper, 'Don't worry. Now see the magic.' And I called out to the owner. 'You don't worry, Sir. This person is very dirty but tell me, are we all human beings? Don't we all have lots of grime within that we don't see outside?' That eatery owner pushed me out. All of a sudden, I offered him money then. 'See. If you allow this man in, I will pay you a hundred rupees for just letting him in.' The owner suddenly stopped pushing me out and smiled, then said, 'I was just joking little boy. You can come in…' Then he asked me, 'what will you like to have?' I laughed at him and then ordered some *chapatis* and *dal* and some vegetables. After filling our stomachs, I asked for the bill. The owner said, 'Hundred rupees for entrance of this old man and ninety rupees for your food.' I gave him two hundred and said, 'Keep the change.' That old pauper and I got out of the restaurant and I told him, 'Okay then, old man. I go towards my unknown destination. Keep these fifty rupees for your next meal.'

I was just about to walk away when the old man said, 'Who are you?' I replied, 'I don't know. Even I'm searching for this answer since my birth.' The pauper said, 'Who sent you, I have no idea. But whosoever you are… you are a nice and kind-hearted little boy and a little, cute son of God.' I just smiled and said, 'No…No, old man. I'm not a son of any God. I'm just an orphan who is wandering about and craving for a family's love.' Then I ran away from there. And then, once again began my trudging towards an unknown destination. I just kept walking down the streets, waiting for some other thing to happen.

෨෬෨෬

Flying Like A Bird

The voice overhead brought me back from my reverie. 'May I have your attention please? The plane is going to land shortly and we hope for another opportunity to serve you in your future journey.' An air hostess came to me and tousled my hair, and with a smile on her face, said, 'Hey sweetie, have you fastened your seat belt?' Then she gave me lots of toffees. The experience was novel. Because as I had sat back, I had travelled back to my past. But my future was ahead of me. Something strange was happening to me in real life. My life had been really pathetic but here, in this airplane, I was getting lots of respect from the air hostesses and from people around me. I looked at all the smiling faces, and I asked myself a question, 'Is this possible? That people are so kind hearted?'

Within a few minutes, the plane landed and we headed

towards the exit gate of the Manila airport. I was shocked. Some people were waiting there with banners in their hands and as they saw us, one lady came forward and hugged me and kissed me. Her name was Cecilia. Cecilia Flores-Oebanda is the Founder and Director, Visayan Forum Foundation (VFF), who is known all over the world for her work on human trafficking. This was the first ever kiss that a stranger gave me. I couldn't believe this had happened to me. There were many many questions bubbling inside me. I was beginning to understand that my existence was important. I kept asking myself one question again and again. 'Am I that special?'

In my entire past life, I had just dreamt of small gestures of love and affectionate conversation. This time, people treated me as if something was really different. Or was this all a dream? I felt fresh and brand new. I felt like I was alive this time. After this caring meeting, we went towards the car which was waiting for us. As we got into it, I was just thinking that, 'Had I been dreaming of this life all the time?' Somehow, I thought the present was a dream. That I was getting VIP treatment, was a dream. To savor the moment, I rolled down the car window and put my head out to take stock of some sort of a tangible reality. Manila's summer air touched my face, blew through my hair. At last, the feeling of being in a dream began to go away and reality began to sink in. I could at last see a beautiful life ahead, where I could free myself from this scary world. I also realised that this world was not all that scary. It was not going to be always as bad as my past life had been.

The car halted before a tall building and my escort and I headed for our room, arranged in a hotel in the building. All I remember today is, I saw a large white bed. I flung myself on it without taking off my shoes. Under the eiderdown, I was so happy. For the first time, I was enjoying myself thoroughly and I wanted to jump around and fly around like a bird. I couldn't because I was human. As I saw the clock, which hung on the wall and went tick, tick, tick...I just stared at it and again went into yet another flashback...

I learnt to dream from the airplanes. They flew higher than birds, taking my dreams higher and higher. I dreamt big. As my heart beat restlessly and at the same time, every little beat brought many desires and wishes to my mind, those huge birds taking off, encouraged me to soar higher and higher. And the landing airplanes taught me the happiness which you get after completion of the journey. As my heart never stopped beating rapidly, so my desires had to take flight and they never halted. Infinite number of dreams flashed in my mind's eye, inspired me to hope to fly in the sky, with that white cloud on its endless journey.

I always had a desire to be on the top. A position from where I could help each and every person on earth. Like a sun, which is out of reach of human beings, but it spreads light on the earth, sustaining life on earth without discrimination and bias.

It was a drizzling summer day. After escaping from Sama's house, I had gone back to the street. To my old gang of friends. It was a beautiful day, warm and wet. The sun was trying to shine through the light rain; trees were taking a bath and there was flashing greenery everywhere; it was a day of romance, nature itself was in love and beautiful. I and my friends were roaming about near the airport. There were lots of people who were coming and going. Fleets of cars were waiting to pick up visitors. We were just loafing around and I was teasing some romantic pair. One couple was very angry with me, so I told my friends, 'let's get out of here.' But my friends were not so ready to leave the airport. I decided not to tease anyone anymore and walked along with my friends. One of my friends said, 'This place is very nice. I think we should come here daily.' Suddenly I saw a plane, which was taking off, I was so happy and smiling, seeing it fly. So I started to think, 'One day, I will be on this airplane and that day will definitely come. Will you help me God? My life will not remain the same for ever. It will have to change...' It was the very first day that I ever saw a plane up from very close. I really liked it because I felt inspired to fly high.

From then on, every day, I used to see the sunset in the airport. I liked to see the flying planes take off and land, the round saffron sun behind them. My friends started to ask me, 'What happened brother, you pass all your time in

the airfield, you don't want to work? And earn any money?'
I gave them very simple and weird answers, 'Don't disturb
me at this moment brother. I am thinking of how to be a
rich man. Be a tycoon, I should know the ways to make
money. So, I'm observing these rich men very closely.' I was
a very small kid and my thoughts were weird. My friends
laughed at me and said, 'You have become mad and really
strange. Nobody can be rich while sitting and thinking. Go
to work, otherwise you will not even get food to eat.' But I
didn't listen to them because I loved to watch the airplanes.

One day, some friends accompanied me to the airport
in the evening. That day really went opposite to the usual.
Suddenly I saw a person who was very attractive and carrying
a small black briefcase. He was alone and stuffing the luggage
into the boot of a car. I don't know what came to my mind. I
went near to him and grabbed the briefcase from the trolley
and ran away as quick as possible. My friends saw me. At
first they were startled, then they followed me.

I jumped across the fence of barbwire around the airport.
I slipped and trundled down the road. I got hurt but I
didn't let go of the briefcase. I got lots of scratches all over
my body. But I quickly picked myself up and ran away to
our secret place and buried the suitcase in the ground. In
the meanwhile, my friends also arrived and they asked me,
'What did you steal from the airport?' I pretended to pant
a lot. Eventually, I heaved a great sigh and replied, 'I have

buried the briefcase. We'll take it out day after tomorrow, alright?' Everyone said, 'Cool.' One of my buddies then said, 'Hey! We got to go there tomorrow too. Otherwise people will have doubts about us.' We all agreed, his idea was good. Next day, we went back to the airport. Some policemen were waiting for us and they caught and took us to a police station. We were frightened and our bodies shook in fear. One cop told the officer in charge, 'Sir, these street kids were roaming around the airport.' Another officer came and asked us, 'Yes, tell me... did you steal the briefcase?' I said, 'No…we don't understand….what briefcase you are talking about?' The cop said, 'Don't worry. You all will spit out the story by night.' Then he gave the order to put us in a lockup.

Inside the lockup, we were very scared. Especially me. I had stolen the briefcase. And it was my first time inside a lockup. I told everyone, 'Fellows! Have you seen movies?' My friends replied, 'Yes, so what?' One of my friends even said, 'You seem to be insane. Why the heck are you asking about movie? It's not the time for entertainment. Can't you see our lives are in danger?' I told them, 'I'm not talking here about amusement. I'm trying to warn you all to not tell them anything about any briefcase. Otherwise, they will hang us to death, like in the movies. In the movies, when criminals accept their offence, they are put in prison for a certain time and then they kill them by hanging till death. So, if you love yourselves, don't tell even one word. Just say no...And no, alright?' Everyone was pretty scared and said, 'We won't tell anything. It doesn't matter how much they bash us up.' At night, two cops came into the lockup and asked us, 'Come on... kids, tell us what you know regarding the briefcase?' We started to cry and told him, 'We don't know anything about it. Please let us go.' One policeman began to flog us with his whip. Everyone began to scream and cry. Other cops too started to beat us with their belts. We couldn't do anything, because if we spat out that we had taken the briefcase, they would have killed us. We thought that, it was better to get flogged by them than to be killed. Whole night they kept us in the lockup. In the morning they said, 'Okay. Now you can go kids. You don't know anything regarding the briefcase.'

We were very happy. We began to walk away from the police station, limping. Everyone was badly bruised. Yet, after we got out of the police station everybody was laughing. Everybody had swollen faces, hands and legs. One friend said, 'Now we need some medical attention.' I said, 'Not to worry about that, you didn't hear what the police officer said? There is lots of money in the briefcase. So we will have a party along with the medication.' We were so excited that we forgot our pains and aches. We just ran towards the buried briefcase when we reached the secret place. And we started to dig it out in a frenzy.

When we took out the briefcase from the pit, we kept turning it up and down, upside down, rolling and flipping it but we could not open it. One of my friends had a knife, so he took out the knife from its sheath and said, 'Guys don't waste time, let me open it.' Then he cut the briefcase with the knife and the magic began.

When we saw the money in the briefcase we went crazy. We were holding bundles of money in our hands and dancing, like real retards. But suddenly my eyes went to the money and I explored it very carefully. My friends were dancing but I realised that the money we had, it might not be real money! It was fake money, because it was in some other currency. Not Nepali money. I yelled out, 'No! This money is counterfeit... it's fake money! Oh! Gosh!' Suddenly everyone froze and within moments, our happiness evaporated. My friends stood, clutching fists full of money, staring at me. One of my friends asked, 'Which money is it?' I wondered, and suddenly something clicked in my mind. I shouted very excitedly, 'I know it!' Everyone was looking at me. I said, 'This money belongs to Hindi flicks. Have you guys seen Indian movies?' Everyone replied, 'Of course.' Ram Kumar replied, 'Oh! Yes, I have seen too in several movies. It means, this money is useless?' I replied, 'That's right. This money is worthless to us. Our sacrifices have gone to shit. Anyway, we have to make sure that this money should not exist anymore. Otherwise, the police will catch us.' Day turned into darkness. It was a winter night. We didn't have enough clothes to cover ourselves, so to escape the cold we often burnt something, like bus tyres.

Kancha went to find a tyre to make the place cosy, because it would be pretty difficult to spend a night without fire. Someone spoke up abruptly, 'Hey boys! What are we going to do with this money?' I said, 'Don't worry. We'll put it on fire, use it to set the tyre on fire.' My friend brought the tyre and we tried to burn it. The tyre was damp, so gradually we started to put the money on fire and the briefcase was full of money. Little by little, we burned almost the whole money. Just one bundle remained and I was about to put that bundle also in the fire. But suddenly, I heard a voice from behind, 'Fellows! What you are doing?' I lifted the bundle of cash and said, 'What to tell you bro, we got some money but unfortunately it was fake. Would you like to have a look?' This friend, who had joined us late, was surprised and eager to hold the bundle of cash. I gave him the money and grinned at him. He held the money and said, 'Hey! It is IC!' I got astonished and wondered what he was trying to say. So I asked him, 'What is IC bro?' He replied, 'IC means Indian Currency. This is the Indian rupee. This money is worth much more to us than any Nepali rupee.'

In my ignorance, I mocked at him, 'Are you crazy or what? This money is fake. It is used in flicks and you can't use it to run for your life...you got that?' He said, 'You guys, come along and I'll show you, the money is useful or not.' We left the burning tyre and then followed him. He took out some money from the bundle and moved towards a shopping complex. When we entered a clothings shop, he told us to choose any outfit I wanted. I was thinking, this chap has gone mad. After that, all our friends chose their desired outfits and our friend who had the money took all our attire to the counter and paid with the same currency to the cashier. We felt like great fools. 'Oh! Shit! We didn't know this money is useful. We burned up the whole money from the briefcase. Otherwise we would have made our life happy. We were full of regret. Even then, we had a lot of fun with what was left. We went to the public bathroom, we took bath, and we wore new branded clothes. Then we ran to our favourite hotel, booked three bedrooms and had a sound sleep. Whole night I kept thinking about that money which we had lost in the fire.

The hotel was booked for three days, we had fun for ten days at a stretch. For three days, we ate whatever we wanted to and slept in the hotel bedrooms. The money lasted us for ten days. With it, we went to the movies, shopping and to the zoo. On these days, we went on bicycle rides. There was a separate cycle for me. The problem was, I was the only one who did not know how to ride a bike. Then, suddenly, I recalled my days as a servant. I had taught a girl called Sama, how to ride a bike. That time, those people did not know I could not ride. Now, I had to ride and race with my friends, and this time I could no longer boast around. When we took the cycles, everyone started to ride. I was holding the bicycle and standing upright, but did not ride. One friend noticed and asked me, 'Buddy, what's up? Why are you not riding the bicycle?' I looked at him and said, 'Actually, I don't know how to ride a bicycle. That's why I'm holding it.' He laughed at me and said, 'It's not a big deal. Just try. I know you will learn within an hour.' I was surprised and said, 'Are you sure if I try for an hour, I'll be able to ride the bicycle?' He grinned and answered, 'Of course, buddy.'

My legs and hands were shaking, even then I tried to ride, but I fell down on the ground along with the bicycle. I got hurt, everyone came to me and surrounded me. One friend asked me, 'Basu, are you all right?' I had little scratches on my calf, I was blowing on them with pouted lips and replied, 'Yes I am alright, but I got a little scratch on my calf.' Everyone laughed at me and started saying, 'Shame on you buddy. You don't know how to even ride a bicycle, what will you do in life? You are useless, bu....' Then a friend said, 'Hey! Guys come on... don't waste time because it is fleeting away. You have to pay rent for the bicycles. Let him learn by himself.' So everyone left me behind, and went for the race.

This moment was very hurtful. My friends had abandoned me because I didn't have the skill to ride a bicycle... At that moment I promised myself that for the rest of my life I wouldn't give anyone any chance to ignore me and leave me behind. 'My challenge starts from right now. I shall always be better than the others.' I just got up and grabbed the bicycle and started to learn by myself. I fell over and over, again and again. But I got up every time and tried to ride. Once, I was able to ride on, but after three or four minute, I again fell down. This time, I fell forward and banged my head on the ground. My face got hurt and nose started to bleed. Even then, I again got up and tried to ride the bicycle. My shirt was stained with blood. But it really did not matter. By the evening, I had learnt to ride the bicycle. It was not just learning to ride a bicycle for me, it was learning how to get accepted among people. I was already abandoned by my family. So I realised that I shouldn't be ignored by anyone in the future. I was small but I could understand what really hurts and turns you inside out.

When my friends returned, I told them, 'Hey! Guys, lets ride for an hour again.' My friends laughed at me and said, 'C'mon man, you have been renting the bike since afternoon, you have not learnt anything, and in one day, you can't learn. You have to come here daily, then gradually, you will learn.' I smiled at them and started to ride the bicycle. Everyone was shocked. 'Hey! Basu, you learnt bicycle in one day! It is amazing.' I again demanded, 'so, are you ready to have one ride?' Every one said, 'Okay, lets have a last half-an-hour ride.' I began slowly, everyone was biking fast, but soon I caught up with them. 'He is too good and very talented, he learnt riding in one day', they all said in admiration.

Since then, I have always been above other friends. If I did not have any talent regarding certain things, I used to develop such skills and try to stand above all others. God created us and everyone is special in this world but people don't understand that, so they compare you with whatever talent they do have. So by chance, if you don't have those skills, then people ignore you. That's why, everyone has to struggle for their existence. I have had to struggle all my life.

ॐ✿ॐ✿

The Slaughterhouse

People think that there is no journey without any goal and destination, but sometimes, this is totally wrong. Actually, the person who doesn't have any purpose also reaches some certain station, from where he or she catches the train and life goes on. It keeps moving on towards uncertain destinations. Sometimes, my inner feelings told me that there is something in this universe which is a certain spiritual power that has written out our each and every action. For instance, sometimes, we try to become something according to our desire but we become something else. Sometimes, we make our plan of action but we can't move according to it. Why? This means, we human beings are uncertain as our lives are uncertain. We all have desire to live a long life and we also figure out and have an approximate idea that we will live for about, say fifty years, seventy years and some people also wish that they live to be a hundred. But there is nobody who can have this guarantee... Like that, my life also didn't have any aim and any goal, any guarantee.

I was just walking the endless roads and streets. During this journey, I had found lots of stations, lots of ways to remain alive and exist in this world. And I do believe that, after collecting different experiences, traveling through a variety of social strata and through different platforms in life's journeys in different contexts, one can call oneself somewhat knowledgeable regarding life, human struggle and the world. As the clock kept running tick, tick, and tick, I was also ambling along, putting my little steps on the lonely and crowded road. I was tired of walking and walking and one day, I sat down on the pavement before a slaughterhouse, to rest. I was sitting on the pavement, leaning my back to a wall, stretching my legs out, in a totally sprawling posture. After a few minutes, I went to sleep and do not know what happened during the time I was asleep.

I went to a dream world where everything was extremely beautiful. I was flying over yellow mustard fields, as far as my eyes could reach. I saw big and giant, pure black boulders lying in the centre of the mustard field. I landed up there and started to piddle from top of the boulder and started to laugh, but suddenly I saw an angel who was looking at me from the sky. So I just zipped on my pants quickly and apologised to her. She said, 'You seem very happy today.'

I replied, 'Hum… hum.' Suddenly I heard a very strong honking and got up. I opened my eyes and then the next moment, I found everything strange around me! I started to rub my eyes. Gradually I got up from the pavement and fumbled in my pockets. I was shocked that I couldn't find any money in my pocket. So I understood that somebody had picked my pocket while I was sleeping and having conversations with an angel in my dream. I was just about to run from that pavement.

Then I heard a voice from my side. Someone was speaking to me. A man was standing at the slaughterhouse door. He called out to me a second time. It was only then that I went close to him. When I reached in front of the meat shop, he asked me, 'You were sleeping on the pavement, alright?' I thought I had done something wrong and said, 'Yes. Actually I was so tired. I lay down just to rest but suddenly I went to sleep.' I also told him that, 'Somebody picked my pocket while I was sleeping.' Then the man asked me, 'Do you do anything? In terms of job…' I just stood upright and phew... then started to think, 'I think I can get a job in this slaughter house. So it is better to ask this man for job.' He again asked me, 'Hey! What happened? Don't you work anywhere?' I replied smartly, 'Well… No. But I am searching for a job.'

He called me in, and as I stepped in, I could see lots of meat hanging from pegs. It was quite a big shop. I was shocked to see dangling dead legs and even one goat head, lying on the table and its eyes were open wide. It was like a scary horror movie scene. It was for the first time that I'd seen so much flesh and spilled blood all around. Suddenly the man — the owner of the shop — started to tell me about the work he wanted me to do. He said, 'Don't worry. I will not make you slit the throats of goats and buffaloes. This is the shop and we just cut the chicken here. For the goat and buffalo, we have another place, that is our slaughter house.' I just nodded and said, 'Alright, Sir.' Then that whole day, I sat in a chair and watched all that had to be done in the shop. The owner asked me for tea, from time to time and it seemed he was very nice. The creepiest task was, he taught me to slit the neck of the hens. His method of teaching was quite simple. He called me near to the hens, held in a coop and told me, 'Go and bring one hen from the front coop.' I went and opened it and caught one hen, then took it out from the coop.

He taught me the method of slitting and said, 'Hold two wings by the left hand and then put it under the left foot, by the other remaining foot, press the two legs of the bird. Then catch the neck by the left hand, then slit it with the other hand in which you have held the knife.' It was very creepy for me. Even then, I did follow his instructions. After slitting the throat of the hen, it still tried to move and shake, but he commanded me, 'Now hold it very tightly, otherwise you will be in trouble. It will flutter around and there will be blood all over you. So, holding it very carefully, chuck it into the cauldron of hot water and cover it with the lid for approximately thirty second. Then take it out. After that, take the feather out. Aright? So you got me, yeah?' he asked. I said, 'Of course, Sir. Each and everything.'

He was very happy because I was learning to work as he wanted. After that, the owner said, 'Now you listen very carefully. In the morning, you have to wake up at 5 am and bring the meat of goats and buffaloes from the slaughter house to this shop. And remember, you have to sleep at night, there only.' I was very afraid that I had to watch the sacrifices of the buffaloes. But, at the same time, I was wondering about transportation. I asked him, 'Okay, tell me one thing, how am I going to bring that much meat?' He replied, 'Don't worry. You will get a bicycle and two containers hanging on both sides.' Then he looked confused and added, 'I am wondering how you will bring it on the bicycle. You are too small to ride.' I convinced him and said, 'Don't worry Sir. I can ride.'

So, at 10 at night, the butcher closed the shop and he asked me to wash the meat cleavers and the choppers. After that, I swept the shop's floor very clean. Then he took out his motor bike and he told me to pull the shutter down and shut the shop. I was just jumping and tried to pull it down but unfortunately, the shutter was too high and I was small.

The owner was standing next to me, suddenly he started to laugh at me and then said, 'Okay...Okay... leave it. You did such hard work to pull it down. Now let me close it as quickly as possible because we got to go home as soon as possible.' After closing the shop, he started the motor bike and asked me to sit pillion. When we reached his home, I discovered, the house of the owner was his home as well as his other slaughterhouse.

When I got off from the bike and stood by the side, I could see the barn next to the house where there were buffaloes and goat pens and by the side of the pens, there was also a place where flocks of hens were cackling. It was the first time I saw several animals and hens together. I started to explore around but that butcher asked me to come along inside the house. So I followed him and we climbed to the second floor. While walking up the stairs, I kept looking at everything around and thought, 'Not bad... This butcher seems to be too rich.' He suddenly called out to his wife and introduced me to her. She asked us to be ready for dinner. My employer asked me to go to the kitchen, along with her, and have dinner.

She told me to sit on the floor of the kitchen and started to serve food. When she put the plate in front of me, I could see the meat curry and rice. I was very happy to see so much food and started to eat restlessly. While I ate, the butcher's wife went out of the kitchen. This was good because I was shy, and preferred to be left alone while eating. At the end of my meal, the butcher came to the kitchen and asked me, 'So, how was the food? Did you like it?' I was happy with the food. I said, 'Sir, the food was wonderful. I never had food like this before. It must have been cooked by the Madam, right?' The butcher's wife was very happy and smiling and told her hubby, 'This lad is so sweet. I like him.' I understood that the butcher's wife craved for praise and I decided that whenever she did anything for me, I would praise her a lot, so my job would be secured.

The butcher then told his wife to show me the place to sleep. So she took me down stair and showed me a room and said, 'This is your room and from here you can take care of the goats and other animals. There was a servant earlier. He also used to sleep here. So this is your room now... alright?' I thanked her profusely and then asked her, 'Madam, I don't understand why the earlier servant left the job. You are such a nice woman who even takes care of servants. He must be a crazy person, isn't it?' She was again very happy and said, 'We treat servants as family members. We give them the same food we eat. You go to sleep now. Tomorrow you have to wake up as the rooster cock-a-doodle-dos and transport the meat from here to the other small slaughter house.'

I went to sleep and was lost in a dream world where I was playing football with other children. There was a huge ground with green grass everywhere and my team was in black dress and the opposition was in white. The ball was spinning on the tip of my index finger and the others were staring at the ball. Once it fell, everyone started to run after it and I was also running to get it. Then, after struggling a lot, I got the ball and started to run off to approach the opponent's goal post. I was just constantly running but I wasn't close to the rival's goalpost. My throat was dry and I was tired, but I had not reached the goalpost yet. Then I stopped and swung my head back. I couldn't see anyone on the field. I was just alone, clouds were swirling around me. There was no ground. I was in the sky with my football.

After a while, a very sharp and white light came towards me from the sun. It was so bright, it was very difficult to see. Even then, I tried hard. My heart was throbbing restlessly. I put my hands up and covered my face, to protect my eyes from the glaring ray of light. I was facing the white beam. I slowly parted my fingers and tried to see the light rays. Finally, gradually, I could see four legs with white shoes and pant legs. The rest of the bodies were hidden in the clouds. Then it became clearer bit by bit. I could see a white suit and finally the faces of both the men. The light was now dimmer. The faces of the men were glittering. I looked very carefully. I recognized one man. He was my Pop. The other was a stranger. They came closer to me and stood upright, smiling at me. I was startled.

I began talking to my father. 'How are you Pop? I

miss you a lot. You went without thinking of me, why dad? Now I am totally alone in this world. Struggling and ambling aimlessly with lots of pain in my heart.' I just kept complaining to him over and over again, regarding my pain and his absence. He kept smiling and listening to me. After a while he smiled and told me, 'Dear Son. You are not a simple child on this earth. You can do miracles in this world. You are like raw iron which is heated and burnt to forge and shape a battle sword which is meant for victory. But remember Son, battle means not a bloody war. You have to follow the path of love. Your combat is always for love. And whenever you fight for love, you will see me around.' I was listening to him but couldn't understand what he meant. Finally, I asked the man beside him, 'So, who are you by the way?' The man smiled and stretched his hand towards my head and caressed it. Then he answered, 'I am your friend who always keeps his eyes on you. People know me as God. But for you, I am your friend. So I'll always help you. You just keep going. I'll show you the right track.' After that, I ran towards them and held them both. I said, 'I love you Pop.' Even as I was told that they loved me too, they said, 'You have to be a brave boy for your entire life.' Suddenly, I heard the rooster's call. I looked around in confusion. Now my dream completely vanished, as the cock kept calling. I got up then and rubbed my eyes and recalled the dream. I ignored the rooster and went back to sleep, hoping my dream would come back. But it did not.

In the morning, it was 6 o'clock when the butcher's wife came and woke me up. She said, 'Hey, you sleep like a log. You didn't hear a single cock crow?' I was still asleep but I didn't have any choice, so I got up from the bed, rubbing my eyes. I followed her and she took me to the tap and asked me to wash my face and said, 'Okay, that is the bicycle with the meat containers hanging on the back on both sides of the carrier. That is what you need to distribute in different shops.' I was surprised and asked her, 'But where to supply Ma'am? I don't know the place,' she said. 'You don't worry about today. The other boy is going along with you to supply the meat. But from tomorrow, nobody will go along with you, understand.'

From that day, I began to take the bicycle and deliver meat from shop to shop. On that first day, I had another boy going with me. He laughed and said, 'Hey, you can't ride the bike?' Of course, I could ride the bike, but this was a very high bike and I was tiny. Also the meat on either side of the carrier was heavy and I had to drag the bike. We pushed the bikes along and he kept provoking me. Finally, I had had enough of his insults. So I caught the left handle of the cycle by my left hand and by the right hand caught the upper chassis, then finally I put across the right leg through the middle gap of the chassis, to the right paddle then started to push by the left leg for speed. After getting the speed, I used both the paddles. I call this style of riding the bicycle, the 'scissor style.'

That day, I became half a butcher myself. We went from shop to shop to deliver meat and I realised that I had a new designation in the butcher shop, which was, 'a meat delivery boy.' After the delivery, I had to get back to the shop. There I had to boil water in the cauldron and had to slit the the throat of hens. After sunset I had to stuff the feathers into sacks and had to go to the garbage bins, situated one kilometre from the slaughter house and dump them. This was my daily task. I did this work for two months.

ဆာ၀ဆ၀ဆ

Liberation

The sprinkling... and every drop of blood agitated me and turned me inside out. Those flickering limbs and quivering bodies taught me to be a human and love all creatures on earth. Every sound that emerged out of pain from every throat that the butcher slit, made me understand that there are souls and feelings in every species and they are meant to live on this earth too. I could hear their talk and their anxieties at the imminent end of their lives, but at the same time I understood that there are people around who enjoy the sacrifices of other lives. So soundless conversation with the wordless species with glittering innocent eyes that lived inside the coops, and noises of the creatures which were inside the pens, led me to flee the slaughter house, and at the same time, it taught me to feel the agony of other creatures.

One day, I was siting near the hen coops. The hens were slowly cackling and looking at me. When I stared into their eyes, something happened to me. I felt bad. I felt they were talking to me. They had very sad faces. They were telling me, 'Hey, are you going to kill me today? Whole day I have seen lots of friends getting killed. May be, I am the one today? Will you slit my throat today?' This question made every hair on my body stand up. I could feel their emotions and feelings. I had killed so many of them. Today, they were asking me lots of questions. I turned my head away, but my questions to myself would not go away. 'What's going on? And what's wrong with me today? What kind of feeling is this?' Then again, I looked at those hens. I felt that each and every hen was requesting me for liberation. I felt, they were talking to me. Their eyes blinked with fear of getting killed. Hopelessness was writ large. They lived with knowledge of their death and quivered with helplessness. After a while, I just got up and opened the coops and said, 'Come on...run. Get out of here... live your lives...' Each and every bird ran out of the coop and scattered hither and thither.

After a while, the butcher saw me and heard my voice. He ran out of the shop, shouting, 'Hey stop it! What are you doing? Come on...stop.' I didn't stop and kept telling the hens, 'Get out of here. Come on... fast.' The butcher thought that I had gone mad. He began to catch hold of as many of the hens as he could and put them back into the coops. He said, 'You idiot! You insane! What have you done? Seven or nine hens have run way because of you. You got that?' I told him, 'I don't want to work here anymore. I can't kill these hens. Give me my salary. I want to quit this job right now.' The butcher was very angry. 'You bastard. What do you think of yourself? You just tried to destroy my business and now you are asking for money? Get out of here! You son of a dump.' He began to hit me with the butt of a cleaver.

I just tried to escape from him. I got injured very badly because the cleaver's butt was not soft. It was of iron. I even tried hard to run and finally, I escaped from him. Then I kept running through one lane to the other, and didn't look back until I was two mile away. When I stopped, my heart was beating. I looked around and sat on the pavement. I couldn't hold my breath. Then, slowly, things settled. I started to think about the mad run, and the entire sequence of event. I did not know why I had let the hens out. What had happened to me? After a while, I looked up at the sky and asked God, 'Hey God, why? Why I have to run for my survival? There is not even a single place where I can live happily and peacefully. Will my life be like this always? I keep hearing that God comes in any form and he always helps miserable people. But when God? When will you come to help me?'

After complaining a lot, I stopped thinking for a while. Then I felt very happy that I had let the hens out of the coop.

I had done a great job. I felt good. I felt great. That was the God in me. I had fought for a good cause. Good feelings are known as God feelings. Bad feelings are known as evil. I might have done lots of bad things. I had to live on the streets and survive. But I wasn't bad by birth. No one is bad by birth. I had been bad because I had been made bad by society. The world had abandoned me on the streets, on an empty stomach, which I had to fill somehow. But goodness had never left me. It had remained as a lotus flower, which grows in dirty water but it never leaves it's prettiness and beauty. Yes, it is very hard to be always a good person because a lot of hindrances come in one's way. For the good feelings emerging within me, I had been bashed up very badly by the butcher.

But it doesn't mean that we should not follow our good feelings. We are human beings and we are meant for love, kindness and righteousness. That's why we are known as human. If we have to weigh the price of being good, I would say, you have to pay for everything in life. For instance, if you are mother or father of a child, you have to pay with your time, your love, you have to work very hard to give a life to your child. The work which you do for your family and earn money is not free. You pay with your physical energy and you burn your blood. When I was a small child, I had heard the story about Jesus Christ. Even he had to pay for his honesty and righteousness. He gave his life for love, kindness and righteousness, with a smile on his lips. I was worried about my next move but I was not actually worried. I knew that my Pop was with God. He would request God to help me. I was really naive, I believed in what I dreamt. But it was really good, because it gave me courage.

శ౦ఁ౪ఁ౦ఁ

Cycle Thief

How wonderful it would be if you could turn night into day, blue to bliss, but we know it's just a dream. It's like we are floating a paper boat in a stormy sea and we are aware that sooner or later, it will drown. As it is, I couldn't change my life from darkness to brightness because it was not within my power to do so. My life was floating in the sea of hopelessness. Loveless and the restless, full of struggles and troubles. Day after day, month after month, I had to go through a new and horrible kind of work just to be able to find food.

It was yet another rainy day. Everything looked green and fresh. But I was shivering and my teeth were chattering because of the cold. I had walked several miles and had reached a tea stall. There were a lot of people gathered around the tea stall, all drinking hot tea. It was still raining. I wanted tea but I searched my pocket. I only had a wet hundred rupee note. I did not know if I could buy tea with that. But the tea stall owner was kind. He dried my wet note on the lid of the tea cauldron, and gave me a glass full of hot tea. As the warm liquid cruised down inside me, I felt somewhat better.

After having the tea, I continued walking again until I reached a bicycle shop. Here, some boys were fixing bicycles. So I halted there, there was some shelter here. I thought of waiting here until the rain stopped. The shop owner noticed me and said, 'Hey! What are you doing here?' I said, 'Sir, it is raining so heavily. I am standing under your shop's eaves, to wait for the rain to stop.' After a while the boys repairing cycles began to have tea. I stood and stared at them. The owner saw me again. This time he smiled at me, then offered me a cup of hot tea and said, 'You seem to be shivering in the cold. So, have a cup of tea.' I was glad to have it because I was really feeling cold. I scrambled towards him and sat down with them to have a cup of tea. While I sipped the tea, they started to question me. 'Hey! What's your name? What you do? Where are you coming from, and where are you going?' I smiled and said, 'You guys seems to be very inquisitive. I have only one thing to say. I am a homeless person. I am the king of the streets. Live on the streets, and I keep rambling down the road to fill my tiny stomach. I need work. So if you guys are really interested in me, then please keep me here with you to work.' The owner of the shop looked at me for a while and then thought, I would work well for him. People who came to the shop to get cycles repaired were often nasty. They complained that the job was not well done and they refused to pay often. I was a street rowdy. I was querulous. And aggressive. The perfect person to tackle nasty customers. The owner warned me, 'You don't worry. You can work here along with the other guys. But before that, I would like to make it clear to you that the work is very hard. You have got to learn it properly from your seniors. Some times, customers are not nice. So you need to speak with them very boldly. I mean...you have to take money somehow after fixing the bicycles, alright?' I was confident and I said, 'You don't worry, Sir. I'll work very hard and will never let anyone get away without paying.'

Days passed. I was learning the work. But I was sick because of the monotonous nature of the work. One day, a friend strolled into the shop. He was my street friend. He was really surprised that I was working in the bicycle shop. We chatted for long. Then he gave me an idea. He said, 'Hey you, dump! You seem to be a fool, working like a donkey. Only a donkey does very hard work.' I was surprised and began to think. Then suddenly, he said, 'Come on... man. You have to get out of here and have to live life like a prince.' I was quite happy. Innocently, I asked, 'How can this be possible?' He grinned and said, 'Now, listen very carefully.

Tomorrow you and I are going to take bicycles from your shop. And after that, we will sell them at a nice price, alright?' I was scared. What if we were caught? He asked me, 'What happened? What are you thinking about?' I stared at him, and said, 'You bugger. You are mad. You don't want me to stay alive in this world.'

He laughed and dared me. 'Oh! My God. Our Hero, who is known as a brave guy, has now became a coward. Not a daring lad anymore. Just a pussycat.' When he taunted me, I became very bold and said, 'Hey! I am the same guy who is never scared. Never worried about my life. I am not afraid of this world. I am the king of the road. I've lived my life with lots of guts and now you shut up. Otherwise, I'll kill you right away... And regarding stealing bicycles... Tomorrow evening you and I will take the bicycles for a ride. After that we'll move to another part of the city to sell it.' After saying this, I returned to my work at the bicycle shop. Next day when I got up, I took out two new bicycles. The owner got out and asked me, 'What are you doing with the new bicycles?' I spoke up very nicely. I said, 'I need to clean them properly because they are a little dusty.' The owner was very happy. He did not suspect anything wrong. I also told him that today I'd go for a ride with my friend for one hour, alright? He was impressed with my honesty. He gave me permission to go riding with my friend. In the evening, when my friend came. We both took the two new bicycles from the shop and ran away towards a place, known as Kothesor. It was near the Kathmandu airport. I started to sweat but I kept paddling hard. My heart was beating fast. My friend asked me a question. But I couldn't hear anything because I was scared and numb. My friend looked at me with a smile on his face and said, 'You are still the same guy, full of guts.'

'I know I have guts and I don't need to prove it to you... but think of the other side of the story. If we get caught, I will be the dead person, not you.' I knew that I was very badly scared inside. To give myself courage, I told myself I was brave. Then I laughed and laughed my guts out. I laughed so much, I almost fell off the bicycle. Instead of getting away quickly, we were laughing and trying to trip each other off the bicycles. Finally we reached Kothesor. Here we stopped then wandered around, to find some place to sell the bicycles. Suddenly I saw a big shop with lots of bicycles around. So my friend got into the shop and I just stood outside. He came out with one fat man. The man looked at the bicycles and said, 'I will pay two thousand for this. If you want to sell, sell. Otherwise you can take them away.' I was scared because they were stolen bicycles. So I said, 'It's okay. Give us the money first.' He looked into my eyes and gave me a really suspicious smile. Then said, 'Here, take it.' That fat man took both the bicycles. My friend then began arguing with me, 'Why did you agree for just two thousand rupees? We'd have got more.' I replied, 'Are you such an idiot. Don't you realise that they were stolen? If he had called the cops, then both of us would have been behind bars.'

'Sorry, I didn't think of that', my friend admitted. Then he put his arm around my shoulder and pulled me closer. We hugged each other and went in search of food. We got into a restaurant after a while, drawn by roasted chicken hanging on long iron skewers. We decided to feast on roasted chicken. I asked my friend to pay, from his share of the money. He said, that was not fair. I pointed out, but for me, there would not be any stolen bicycle, nor any money. He finally agreed. 'Don't ever dare to mess with me alright?', I told him and laughed. My life had again taken a dramatic turn, thanks to my friends. I had become a bicycle thief. I was jobless and on the street once again.

સ૦૦૨૬૦૦૨

Where The Heart Is

Once again, I began to think what to do next. I kept walking with my friend. Talking. 'Hey! Do you remember Kumar, Kancha, Ram, Phuchche, Lama, Padam, Ghaite, Gurung and Bhote?' Of course, I remembered them. We were a team. 'They took care of me. I also remembered Bali who saved me once when I was almost dead. These people were the people who saved me.' My friend Mussa replied, 'I know. Even I'm in your team, you know that and don't think about our favours to you. You too have helped us a lot by picking pockets and your life has been in danger many times.' While walking and talking, we reached our old point of rendezvous, under the familiar bridge. All my friends were gathered there. They were having a party. Everybody was high. Some were having weed and some were drinking. We had just arrived. They saw us and set up a clamour at once. 'Basu and Mussa!!' They started to laugh and hug us. Some of them were just crying and saying, 'Where were you all these months? We missed you a lot.'

It was one of the happiest moments of my life. I had met my friends after a long time. I told them, 'Okay chums. Whatever you want to have, just feel free, because the party will be on me!' We were rich at that moment. I gave a thousand rupees to Phuchche. As he held that much money in his hand, he said, 'Oh! My God! This is a lot. Thank you so much...' Some of the guys went to bring some more bottles of booze and food. The others made place for us to sit. People generally party in posh and aesthetic places. We were sitting under the bridge, close to a dirty drain. We were burning three-wheeler tyres to stay warm. Yet, we imagined a campfire and we just sat and talked. For music, there was the honking of passing vehicles. Yet, we forgot all the pain and worry, each one of us smiled. Some people had slurred speeches, they had drunk too much. But who cared? We were hell bent on enjoying ourselves. We were just living and feeling alive each and every moment. Suddenly Phuchche spoke up, 'I really miss my Mom and Dad, whenever I see children of my age along with their parents. I envy them and something really goes bad in my heart. It really makes me feel pain inside. It's like someone is pinching me hard inside.' Then he started to cry... and everybody started to pacify him. I was a brave boy. I did not cry. My Mom? My Pop?

Phuchche

As strange as the name he had, his story was stranger than and more painful than mine. The name Phuchche was given by the gang, because in Nepali slang, Phuchche means small. When he was around one year old, Padam and Bhote found him in the landfill when they were rag picking. They saw this small boy without name, just sitting in the garbage bin and saying nothing. They picked him up from there because they also had no friends. So they were happy to find the new one. As Phuchche grew up, he was really good at begging and he liked to dance whenever he passed by any places where music was on. He would smile and just start to dance immediately, until the music was over. One day, when we saw a marriage procession we followed them and to a wedding hall. As we reached there, we heard the Nepali traditional music. Phuchche ran towards that marriage ceremony hall, but he was not allowed entry. We were sorry for him. We could hear the music outside the banquet hall too. So, as the music started, he began his moves. It was like he was born to dance, each and every step and all the moves were so nice. People made a circles around and started to smile as he was smiling while dancing. That day I realised that he felt some sort of calmness while dancing. He was trying to override the pain which he had in him, because I could see him smile with each step. It was as if there was a fire burning in him and he was trying to quench it through music and dancing. Whenever I thought of him I really felt good for him because at least, he could dance and smile. There were so many who would have died in the waste bin, without a smile.

Whenever he was drunk, Phuchche would cry. One day, he asked me, 'Basu brother. Who are my Mom and Dad? Why did they leave me in that garbage bin?' He used to ask me these questions and hug me. I had only one answer for him. Even I'm searching for my mother and who she was. Who was my father? The party went on despite the crying and emotion charged conversation. People drank more and more. As the bottle passed around, I could see Bhote right beside Phuchche, who was laughing like a mad man. He smoked weed and even laughed at Phuchche's sadness.

Bhote

Bhote had a really different story. He used to tell us that he was the product of alcohol because his dad was a chronic alcoholic. He had a step-mother and two step-sister. They never treated him like their own. He was always discriminated against by their dad, step-mother and step-sisters. He used to cry whenever he missed his mother. One day, he had shouted at his step-sister, for misbehaving with him. His father beat him up brutally and kicked him out of the house. Since then, he had been in our gang. He was really the experienced one. Once he got an opportunity to get into an orphanage, but he was so violent and short tempered, that when he had an argument with one of the staff of the home, he thrust a knife at the man and ran away. In fact, it wasn't the first time that he had used a knife to stab someone. It was his daily fight. Other children were always scared of him because he used to believe in stabbing, rather than talking and arguing with someone.

Once I asked him, 'Why did you leave that orphanage? You used to get free food and education. And one day, you would have become a really educated person.' He scoffed at me and said, 'You don't know anything about orphanages. They had free food but that was their business. They never treated us right. They used to treat us like we were some sort of diseases. And we had to tell our stories over and over again to people. People were doing studies on us, like we were some kind of research subjects to study. Warden and staff used to punish us severely, as if we were some sort of criminals. There I felt like I was more discriminated against than by my step-mother. It is true that you get free food and accommodation and some sort of normal education too. But they never treat you as their own children. When visitors came, we had nice clothes and good food. Then, suddenly, the staff pretended that they had forgotten even their own children and were sacrificing their whole life for us.

'Small children were also victims of sexual abuses by the

older children. I still remember the day when I had a scrap with one guy. So they came along in a gang and took me to the toilet. Then they sexually abused me, one by one. I couldn't do anything because they pointed a knife at me. The next day, I tried to complain about those guys. But the warden punished me because those children were his favourite ones. This was the reason that I stabbed him and ran away.' Ever since, Bhote was never scared of anyone because he used to tell me, 'Why should we be scared? Whatever bad could have happened, it has already happened to me and several times I have been almost dead in gang fights. So I don't have any more fear in me.'

Suddenly Kanchcha threw an empty bottle in the fire and Padam jumped away as a piece of sticky burning tyre sprang at him. Everybody was drunk. Mussa splashed liquor on the tyre to extinguish the fire. But it got stronger so we tripped down to Padam and started to kick at him to put out the flames on his clothes. Finally, we saved him. It was really funny for each and every one, because at that moment, we felt a sense of the heroic and adventure. Each and everyone started to laugh because Padam's face was really horrified. We started to roll on the ground and started to laugh our guts out. Padam couldn't say anything because he was still scared. When I looked at his frightened face, I remembered his story.

Padam

Padam was one of my friends, yet I always had fights with him. All of my friends used to call him Padam. I used to pronounce it Paadam, which means fart, so he would fight with me. But I was also the guy who never changed and stopped teasing him. Padam was born in the slums near the river Bagmati. His dad was ill and could not work and his mom did nothing. Padam used to be a rag picker and his small sister used to beg around Thamel. Unfortunately, these two, brother and sister, had to take care of their parents. Sometimes, the day would be bad. No earning. In those times, Padam used to be very worried because by the end of the day, he had to get some money to get medication for his dad and food for the entire family. It was really not an easy life for the eight-year-old tiny little boy, just a little older than I was. Padam had a lot of mental tension. He indulged in drug peddling to make some money, he used to peddle cannabis and marijuana but he also became an inveterate drunk. Then one day, his father died. And his sister disappeared from the street. He tried to search for her everywhere for days and days, but there wasn't a single trace of her in any place he knew.

A few years later, when Padam had grown up a little, he started to visit prostitutes. He went there with older friends. One day, such a visit turned him inside out. One day, when he entered the shanty of a prostitute, he found his mother standing in front of him and taking money from another client. That day he left the slums and his home and just started to sleep under the flyover. He called himself an orphan and he never visited his mom again.

Suddenly Mussa tapped my shoulder and asked me, 'What are you thinking?' I answered, 'Just thinking about you guys and I'm so happy to see you all smiling and laughing, because we have lots of pain inside and each and every one has a different agony, but we don't care. We just move on in life as if nothing ever has happened to us.' Kumar asked me to have a bottle of beer but I really didn't like the taste, so I refused, 'No. Thank you very much,' I said. But Kumar insisted and finally, I had half of the bottle and got really high. I do not remember when my eyes closed.

ॐ૭ॐ૭

Now A Baker

I had met my old street friends, gave them a party and had a nice time. Gradually, the money from the stolen cycle vanished. Then I started to think what to do next. I couldn't figure out what was it that I could do without being tortured. I could not work in another slaughterhouse or be a servant again. I was just moving around from place to place, I just kept wandering for a few days. Finally I saw a factory which was a bread-making unit and I went there and asked for a job. A man was standing outside, I asked him, 'Is there any job for me?'

The man who was standing in front of me was startled and asked me, 'What job can you do, young lad?' I immediately replied, 'Any type of job. I can do it but tell me one thing, will I get a job here or not?' The man in front of me was surprised by my style of talking and told me, 'You young lad, you seem to be very hard and harsh. But any way, I like you. I will ask my owner, you stay here, alright?' I was very impressed with that person because he intended to help me.

After fifteen minutes, he came out and said, 'You don't worry, little lad. You will get a job here. Come on... come with me, our owner wants to meet you.' I went along with him. The boss was sitting on a chair. When he saw me, he asked me, 'Hey! You little lad, you are very small. Will you be able to do the work here, in this factory?' I was a little annoyed by his assumption that I was too small to work. I replied, 'You see, Sir, don't think I am small. I can do any type of work, whatever you will tell me to do. But the thing is, I am an orphan lad sleeping on the streets. I don't have any dwelling place. So please give me accommodation along with the job.'

He grinned and stared at me and said, 'You are much bolder than your years, and I really like your... style, don't worry, you can sleep in our factory.' I was very happy. I said, 'Thank you, Sir. But you didn't mention my salary.' He looked at me very strangely and in astonishment and said, 'Salary? What salary?' I looked at him and said, 'All these men working here, are they all working for free? You don't give them money?' He laughed and said, 'Okay! I understand. How much salary do you want?' I was a little surprised because it was the first time that some owner had asked me how much salary I wanted and not told me how much I would get. My mind went into a whirl. Suddenly the boss asked me, 'What happened?' I replied, 'Nothing, Sir. Just thinking, how much should I ask? Because I have absolutely no idea, what work I would have to do here. That is why, I got a little confused.' He then said, 'Okay, I'll give you two hundred rupees per month, fine? And you are a very smart guy at this pretty small age. I have never met such a glib talker. My little son is your age and your height. He is not as sharp as you are and your boldness is mind-blowing. Tell me one thing, if one well-built hefty guy came to you to beat you, what would you do?'

I answered him directly, 'Sir, I would kill him. Doesn't matter how powerful he is.' The boss scoffed and said, 'Interesting. Okay. You may go now.' I was very happy and showed the owner my deep gratitude, 'Thank you very much, Sir. This is enough for me... with food and accommodation.' After meeting with the owner, I walked towards the gate and went to the same man to whom I had spoken first and said, 'Hey! Old man, listen to me. That owner said you are going to explain to me what I have to do here. So, okay, tell me what I have to do.' The first man took me to the baking room where they baked the breads. It was evening time, so everyone was very busy. I took a look around and I could see some people were emptying the bread moulds and some were kneading flour to make the dough. I was surprised that they were jumping on the dough with bare feet and some people were fixing the oven, for baking the breads.

My work was to clean the whole factory and pack the breads into plastic covers and take them for delivery. There was a small rickshaw for me to deliver bread. I had to go from shop to shop and home to home to deliver these packets of bread. It was quite a tough job for me. However, I had decided that I would do this kind of hard work, rather than do a 'bad' job and spend my time in bad company.

I was still very small and it was hard work. I did not have a single minute to roam around and relax. After some time, I got totally frustrated with my job. So I decided to leave it. But I couldn't talk to the owner because the owner used to visit the factory only once or twice in a month. So I continued working there for three months. Then one day, I asked to factory's watchman to call the owner and ask him to give me my money. I told him, I was fed up of the work. He told me, 'Okay. Don't worry. Whenever the owner comes, I will let you know and you can go and speak to him.'

Fortunately, I was very lucky. The very next day, the owner visited the bakery. I scrambled to him and said, 'Sir, I'm tired of working here. So, I want to leave now. Could you give me my money?' He was a very nice person. He said, 'Okay. Take a thousand rupees, alright?' Then he took out a thousand rupees from his pocket and gave it to me. When I got that money in my hand, I was very happy because it was the first time that I had money in my hand that you could say, I had earned after roasting myself before blazing ovens for three months. In my whole life, I had never felt so satisfied. It was my hard earned money, the fruit of honest labour. I told the owner, 'Thank you, Sir.' Then I got out of the factory. They say, once a wanderer, always a wanderer, and I was growing up to prove that true.

ॐ॰ॐ॰

Call Of The Street

*T*he journey of life is really mysterious, you attempt to jaunt along a course you think you have planned, but you reach somewhere else, because there are different tracks for different destinations and various crossroads and junctions, which often takes you to a different world. Different lives cross your path, but you never know when you trail the right track. Some wise man said, 'Everything happens for the best', but this is not completely true. Nature has different rules and it needs time and period to change, so the intermittent period can be for good or bad, it depends on nature — how it reacts and for this reaction we have various terms like fate, destiny and fortune.

Time: It is meant to change and nobody can convert according to his/her own comfort or convenience. No one can stop the ups and downs, which come in our lives. This *is uncertain; but changes of time are certain. So we can try to do the right action, to change a few scenarios in our lives. Living in the confinement of changing times of nature itself could create a new world for our lives. As we confine ourselves inside of the time cycle, we can't change the time, but we could change scenes of our lives, which might bring happiness in the distant future for the whole life.*

It is true that each and every beautiful picture comes through the dark negatives. So, if your days are deadly dark and you are not able to grope at your future, you need to calm down at that moment, because God might have some strategy for you. He might be trying to make things brighter and create a happier world for you. Just as we develop a colourful picture out of a dark negative roll, so does the brightness unroll from the darkness of desperation.

When I got out of the factory, I felt like the king of the world. Wow! What a great relief, not to have to take orders, not to have to work. A calmness came over me. I felt lighter and lighter. I was just taking off on an imaginary flight of fancy. I was just walking down the street but I felt like a free bird, fleeting from hill top to hill top, soaring up and above; higher and higher like I was touching the cloud which was drifting as casually as I was walking up and down the streets, from street to street. I wanted to share this happiness with someone of my own. Suddenly, I missed my Pop.

I went to the highway, which was very far and completely isolated. I couldn't see even a single person on this road, but I kept walking on and on. Gradually the day turned darker and the twinkling beauties we call the stars came out and the sky was decked as a bride. After a long journey, walking many miles, my legs gave up. I saw a big milestone. Then I sat down on it and started to think about my Pop. I again looked up at the bejeweled night sky and searched out the star which was the brightest. I saw this one star, which was twinkling brighter than the others. That was my Pop. I kept looking at it and started to have a conversation with it and said, 'Hi! Pop, how are you today? See, your son has earned a thousand rupees after working so very hard for three months. Are you feeling happy for me?'

I kept sitting under the night sky, talking, 'Where are you Pop? Why don't you just appear like magic and hug me? I also need a lap to put my head on. And I need a hand to caress me when my heart aches. Can you feel that dad? I don't have even a small house where I can stay. There is no mattress and quilt to cover my body in this killing winter. I am like a dog which struggles the whole day for food and takes the corner of the pavement and goes to sleep. You know Pop, whenever I see children getting loved by their families, I feel very jealous of them. When somebody hits them or beats them, their mom and dad come to their support. And if, suddenly, they fall ill, their parents get worried. But look at me dad. Where are my parents to look after me? Where is that part of my love and affection which was meant for me? I am also a human being, Pop. I also get hurt and have a human heart which aches at times. I also have feelings inside of me. I am not a dead stone dad.'

I said, 'Your God is very selfish. He never feels the human heart and he doesn't know what is good. And what is bad. He can't judge properly. If he was a nice judge, he would have understood who needs whom and what. People say that, "God knows everything". Then why doesn't he understands that I need you dad? More than him. He is God. And he can get everything, whatever he wants within a snap of fingers, because he is the Almighty. He has magical power but I don't have it. I am very simple and an ordinary human being. A very small, helpless and tiny child. So leave my dad and send him to me. I beg you please God...'

It had been really a strange day. I had experienced two aspects of emotions, like the two sides of the same coin, which was getting flipped by itself. In the morning, I had been so happy. I could see life in all its really myriad hues. When day turned into darkness, my heart started to ache and I started to weep. I cried and sobbed but nobody heard me. Neither my dad, nor the God I was just looking for in the vast sky overhead, and talking to, just like I was talking to all the blinking stars. After crying like mad and letting all the pain inside me out, I sat on that isolated highway, all by myself, feeling empty and somehow clean. Without any grief inside of me. I felt very relaxed then. Slowly, after a long while, I got up from the milestone on which I had sat.

Then I put my small, small steps towards the city road. I turned towards the city, kicking and playing with a small tin coke can. After many slow and aimless hours, I reached the street where my friends lived. They were fast asleep under the bridge by that time and by their side, a warm fire blazed. When I reached there, I woke everyone up and gave them a surprise. Everyone got up and began to ask, 'Oh! How come you are here?' It was around 5 o' clock in the morning. We had an hour's conversation. In the mean time, we warmed our hands and it was soon dawn, and 6 o'clock. Then one friend said, 'Come on...! Let's have tea.' Everyone left the shelter of the flyover and went to the tea stall. All of us had very warm and pleasing tea. It was a very cold morning. When we spoke, we could see vapour coming out of our mouths, after the tea. It was a fresh new morning. I had cried and walked all night. I had not slept.

Lama started to fumble in his own pocket, for some money. Unfortunately, he didn't find anything. Everyone got into a panic, for the bill for the tea had to be paid and the boys started to fight and abuses each other. Suddenly Lama shouted, 'Who the hell picked my pocket? I'll kill that ba...' I began to laugh loudly and everyone went into a pin drop silence and stared at me. Mussa then asked me, 'What happened?' In a very astonished way, I replied, 'Who would dare to steal money from a pickpocket?' Then, they too started to laugh, pointing out with their index fingers at Lama. The tea stall owner got angry because all of us were laughing and we had not paid him yet. He began asking for money for the tea we had drunk. Suddenly Kumar shouted out and said, 'Run...Run away....' Then everyone started to run. I shouted out to them, 'Stop.... Stop...you don't need to run away. I'll pay it.'

All my friends were very happy now. The owner of the tea stall was the most happy. Then I paid the tea bill. Even after paying the bill, everyone kept shouting and laughing, 'Run away.... Runaway....' Then again, Ha! Ha! Ha! The day was perfect and enjoyable... but you see, days do not remain the same. Time never stops at one point. It has to go on. As it is, my life had to take another turn. Everyone started to ask me, what had I done for the last three months? Etcetera...etc. I told them each and everything that had happened to me in the past three months. All about working at the bakery. They were very happy to hear this, but now I had to think what to do next.

Some friends proposed, I return to picking pockets. Some suggested I join a robber gang. But I refused to do any of these jobs because I wanted to do something nice. Finally, after considering one by one everything I had done and many new propositions, one friend told me, 'Don't worry. You can decide whatever you want to do. Until then, we are here to help you out and feed you.'

ജ‌ര‌ജ‌ര

Battling For Bread

B *e strong as a stone. Your body should be iron, and your each and every nerve has to be made of steel, because you need to bear the hardest blows and kicks to fill your empty stomach. Or to get success and not be knocked out in the arena of life. Your glittering eyes must be as red and boiling as lava, and your ears ought to be as active and sharp as the blink of your eyelids. Then only can you fight for your existence. Yet, because you are human, your heart should be soft like water, something no one can catch and control, so that you can spread your love throughout the world.*

After finishing all my money, I began to wander about. My friends were all engaged in the various things they did to earn their living. I was totally at crossroads. I did not have any intention of joining back the gang, so, finally, I chose to work in a hotel. It was a winter morning. I saw a hotel where lots of people were eating different dishes. I thought that, 'If I get a job here, I'd have a chance to eat a variety of dishes, plus, I'll get a salary too.' This work is the 'perfect' job. 'And the money which I'll earn, it will be my hard-earned money.' With such imagination, I put forward my step towards the hotel. Boldly, I went up to the owner. He asked me, 'What do you want?' I replied, 'Well... Sir, I'm searching for work. Will you keep me in your hotel?' He looked at me from top to toe and said, 'You seems to be nice boy. Okay, tell me what you can do. Would you able to wash dishes and wipe the tables?' I answered with a smile, 'Of course, Sir.'

He was also very happy because he wanted a small boy who could do the whole work at the hotel. He knew very well he could take more work out of me than from other older employees. He was very happy to get a helpless boy. Cheap labour. He took me to the inner room where all the utensils were washed. He explained to me each and every thing in detail and told me, 'At night, 12:00 am is the closing time of this hotel. After that you have to sleep in this hotel. Only then, early in the morning, at 4 am, you have to get up and you have to finish all the cleaning work by 6 am. Alright?' I was shocked to hear that I was not going to sleep any longer. However, I thought, 'This is better than working in a bad sector. I prefer to do hard work rather than to steal or pick pocket or beg.'

Everyone who came to that hotel was covered totally from head to toe. They wore jackets, shoes, muffler, gloves and winter cap. But I had to be in slippers, half pant, and a very thin jacket and with bared hand. I had to clean each table very carefully, because customers would drop food all over and spill gravies and water. After a customer ate, I had to collect all the plates and glasses and take them to the washing room. Whenever I washed the utensils, my hands would get frozen and numb. There was a certain compulsion and little choice. One day there was a crowd and great rush in the hotel. I was all alone, to serve the people, I had to run from one table to another.

There was water on the ground. Somehow, I stepped on it, slipped and fell down. I broke four tea glasses and people who were sitting on nearby chairs exclaimed, 'Oh! Be careful Little Master.' I got hurt very badly, my back had hit the floor. I was in great pain. But the hotel owner shouted at me very cruelly, 'Hey! You ba.... you broke four tea glasses. It wasn't your father's property, you got me? Okay come on... now you get up.' He started to beat me. I kept begging for my life, saying, 'Please forgive me. It will not happen again,' My voice did not reach the hotel owner's ears. I kept apologising and pleading for my release but he kept bashing me. It wasn't a matter of some huge mistake, it was just a matter of four tea glasses which cost about three rupees each. At that time, I felt totally helpless. 'A child who is very weak, tiny and insecure.' At that moment I realised that if you don't have power, this world can do anything with you. But if you have power, nobody dares to even touch you. As long as I belonged to a gang, I had never been bashed up by anybody. If someone beat me up a few times, I then had the power to avenge, I had friends and power. But here, in this hotel, I was beaten brutally and I was just crying for my life. But on other hand, I also thought that I was born alone. Which meant, I had to fight alone too. This world is a boxing ring, anyone against me is my foe, and I am the champion of this battle. At the first opportunity to escape, I ran away from this hotel.

Once again, I began to wander. I just walked along but I had no idea where I was going. Things had not changed much. Days passed. I did not earn anything. I had been starving for three days. Without any intention and purpose in my mind, I took a bus for Veerat Nagar. This is a place situated near the border of India. After traveling for long hours, I got to Veerat Nagar. When I got off the bus, I could see lots of people. Some were Indian and some were Nepali. I was wandering and searching for food. I saw a bus conductor who held a lot of money in his hand. I went close to him and asked, 'Hi! Brother. Will you give me some money? I'm very hungry and for a few days I have not eaten anything. Please help me.' He gazed at me very strangely, as if it was for the first time someone had asked him for a few bucks, to eat.

Then, quickly he spoke up, 'Well...I can give you money if you want; do you really want to have money?' I thought, maybe, God had heard my inner voice. I replied hastily, 'Yes bro, I really need the money. For three or four days I haven't eaten.' He grinned at me and said, 'Well... How much do you need? Is five bucks enough for you?' I knew that in five bucks my stomach wouldn't be full. Yet, I thought, beggars have no choice. So I said, 'Okay bro, that's enough.' He called a boy who was very fat and chubby, then said, 'Okay, then dear. You have to fight with this boy. If you win, then the money is yours. If not, then bye... Actually, don't mind. Everybody has to do work and earn money. So, you have to fight with this boy, if you want to take these five bucks. Are you ready?'

I was thinking about it, because I knew that I could not attempt to fight with that boy. I knew that there was no chance of winning this fight but even then, it whetted my appetite. I was ready to clash with him. That lad was very happy to see a smaller, weaker than him and thinner rival. The bus conductor was looking at us and suddenly I heard his voice, 'Come on... fight.' Immediately that lad caught my neck and dragged me forward. I lost balance and fell down. People started to gather at the spot where we were fighting; my mouth and nose were bleeding because I got knocked down and had fallen on my face. That conductor was sitting and encouraging his friend and said, 'Come on...buck up, knock him down.' The lad was so strong, he kicked and punched. I felt giddy and couldn't hit him. At last I fainted. I don't know what happened after that. Everything was blanked out for me at that moment. When I regained consciousness, I found that there wasn't even one single person around me. I tried to turn my head around but it pained severely; my shirt had turned red with blood.

For a while I didn't know why I was there. So I looked at my shirt very carefully. My nose and lips ached and had swollen badly. Then suddenly I recalled, 'I was fighting with someone, where have they gone?' I was also very hungry. I sat at the same bus stand and sobbed, recollecting the whole scene. I had lost. I felt inferior. I could not win even a loaf of bread for myself. It was a twisted, complicated moment in my life. Till now, I haven't got any answer. I felt, we were like some sort of savage dogs fighting for a single piece of bread. There was one bread and many dogs. Each dog applies its whole strength but at last, one dog is be able to take that piece of bread and the rest of the others just keep gazing at the winner dog, with the hope to get it in the future.

What I felt was, every human being struggles and fights for his life. God created us to do great effort and to know pretty closely this whole earth. At least, normal grown up people know the world and are ready to fight to cope with their problems. But what about me? I had not made any

mistake. I was a tiny kid, tussling with this world. I did
the best I could but I got squeezed like a lime, which is, in
between someone's fingers. What remained is the shrunk
pulp and the layer of skin. From the time when I began to
understand things I kept hearing that, whatever sins people
do here on this earth, they would be punished for these in the
next birth. It is right that people should be chastised when
they have knowledge of their sins. If God was punishing
me, then it was by mistake, because I had also heard that
children were pure and innocent. There are people who also
say that children are forms of God. I was also a six-seven-
year-old child. I was also extremely innocent. I was by the
same logic, a form of God. Or the 'future' of the country.
But I was cursed at such a tiny age. No point thinking so
much. Trying to find answers. I left the bus stand. I started
walking — my usual saunter in search of food. My head
ached severely but I kept walking. Suddenly I saw a *dhaba* (it
is the thatched eatery found usually on Indian roadsides). I
halted there and asked for food. Seeing my bloodied clothing
and battered face, the owner said, 'Sorry! I can't help you.
Please go ahead.'

Again I requested him and said, 'Please give me food...
for three days I haven't eaten even a single piece of bread. If
I do not eat today, I will die... please.' I kept pleading with
him. He kept saying, 'No...No.' Then at last I said, 'If you
offer me four *roti*s, I'll wash all your utensils.' He stared at

me for a while, then said, 'Okay. Then you sit. I'll give you food. Instead of four *rotis*, you'll get eight but you have to wash all the utensils till evening, alright?' I was incredibly happy and replied, 'Okay. I'm ready to wash.' Then I sat on the bench and he gave me *roti* and *dal makhani* which is a very famous gravy in Nepal and India. I felt a lot of pain while eating, but I was extremely hungry. So I concentrated on eating rather than thinking about pain. After I finished eating, I felt very relaxed and calmed. I felt drowsy and I wasn't in the right frame of mind to work.

But I had given my word to that hotel owner. So I asked the owner, 'Where are your utensils sir? And anyway, thank you very much for the food. God bless you.' He gazed at me for a while and said, 'Okay. Can you see the container along with the tap?' I replied, 'Yes sir... I can see it.' He told me, 'Go and wash all the utensils.' I was washing for about half-an-hour, when I heard a voice from behind. 'Hey Lad! It's okay now. Thank you very much, you have been working for a long time and you wished me. You told me, "God bless you." Thank you very much for praying for me and I'm exploiting you.' I don't know what had happened to him. He became very sentimental. He seemed to be very inquisitive also. He again asked, 'What happened to your face? You are totally bruised.' I told him everything. Then he felt sorry for me and asked me, 'So, do you have some money.' I was very astonished and stared at him for a while. He waved his hand before my eyes and said, 'Hey! Little boy. I am asking you?'

I answered, 'No sir, I don't have a penny.' Then he called me to his cash counter and took out some money from his counter then gave it to me. It was two hundred rupees. He said, 'Now, perhaps, you will reach your destination boy.' I was quite happy and showed my gratitude, 'Thank you very much sir, may God bless you.' He smiled and answered back, 'Okay, okay...doesn't matter, bye.' I too waved my hand and bid him good bye, 'Bye, Sir.' After that, I returned to the bus stop and took a bus back to Kathmandu.

ഇഗ്ഥൽ

Turning Point

So, once again, I began trawling the streets alone, and just thinking of what to do. All the money I had earned at the bread factory had vanished long ago and I had no new way to earn again. It was then that I fell ill. I was so ill for days that one day, I became unconscious. And this was the most lucky day in my little life. My illness became the turning point of my life. You can say, a nice and beautiful dawn had been calling me, eager to embrace me and my fate kept loudly reciting, 'You have struggled a lot and seen lots of dreams. So, here I am before you once again. I will now put you on the right path so that your dreams are all fulfilled. Once on this path, you will inhale the fragrance of knowledge, and understand the meaning of life. You will be inspired by lots of innovative thoughts and the next years in your life will be a journey of learning and teaching.'

As I lay unconscious on the street, some activists from an orphanage were passing by. Fortunately, their eyes went to me and they admitted me in hospital. It was yet another very lucky day of my life, because I didn't die on that day. As I recovered in hospital, I had a lot of time to think. It was really strange to think about my past life. *Whenever I am about to die, or I get trapped in a dangerous situation, I overcome it by some extraneous intervention. An outside factor comes in and lends a helping hand. Saves me. Every time I am on the brink of death, someone protects me. And this someone is, most often, not even an acquaintance. This puzzled me. It made me ponder about the mysterious being called God. I thought there must be something very important that he wants me to do. Behind his graceful desire to keep me alive, there must be a reason. Maybe, HE wants some sort of a miracle to happen in this world through me. But, so far, I have never figured out what he wants from my life and never understood how he wrote my fate. Whatever path I have followed in my whole life so far, I had just moved on without worrying about the consequences. I had just kept going and going. I had never turned back in my life. I had always just moved ahead.*

৶෮ঔ෮

Orphanage

The story of how I landed in an orphanage is yet another strange tale.

Orphanage is a very common word in this world. Everyone knows that the house, where orphan children live, is called the orphanage. Yet most people are very far from the pain and feelings of orphans, they don't ever think of orphans, if they can help it. There are very few people in this world who have indeed tried to understand the feelings and emotions of an orphan. There are three kinds of people in this world. Most people I have met have different thoughts about orphans. Whenever they meet them or they think about the word orphan, they have negative thoughts for them. They think that orphans are a nightmare, they are horrible, terrible and children who are full of violence. That they are beasts or devils in human forms. Another sort are *people who have kind feelings for these children. Whenever the word orphan comes to their mind, they are full of sympathies for such children and they say, 'Oh! My God! They are very poor... I am so... sorry for them. May God bless them.' And whenever they get the opportunity, they try to donate a little money to the orphanage and other social NGOs; they donate whatever they can.*

And then, again, I have met a third sort of people, who befriend orphans or start to share each and every moment of an orphan's life. The children become very friendly with them and share their life stories with these adult friends. This generally happens in a non-government and government social welfare setup. An orphan child's life story then gets recorded by students and social workers involved in welfare programmes. After the stories are recorded, welfare organisations or governments running orphanages, create projects and send them to different donor or funding agencies. The projects help visualise the feelings and emotions of children. And now there are people, who cry when orphan children tell their stories. They really want to help orphan children. Sometimes, they sponsor the children and guarantee their education. They treat the orphan child as their son or daughter. Sometime it is not possible to adopt from NGOs, because of rules and regulations that bind NGOs. My belief is, humanity is not finished yet, because there are people who help children without having any self-interest, and they possess the same feelings for orphans as they have for their own children.

The NGO that had picked me up from the streets of Kathmandu was called Child Workers in Nepal (CWIN). This pioneer organisation in Nepal was established in 1987 and it works for the rights of the child and against child labour exploitation. CWIN is an advocate agency for child rights, with focus on children living and working under the most difficult circumstances. CWIN's main areas of concern are child labour, street children, child marriage, bonded labour, trafficking of children and it's founder president is Gauri Pradhan. He was a very good friend of mine. Whenever I used to fight at the rehabilitation centre, he used to call me and explain to me about the importance of my talents and of my existence. I still remember the words he said, 'I have worked for many children. They all are very special for me, but sometimes I give more importance to you because you have compassion for your other friends when they are in trouble. And you always take the issue of child labour very seriously. And on the stage, when you talk about child labour you compel people to think and wonder how can such a small child speak in such an intense way? It's hard to believe that you are just a child. So try to understand how important you are and don't underestimate your talent, which is your inbuilt power.' I used to be happy to see Sir Gauri around, and sometimes, he would come especially to meet me and he never forgot to bring chocolates for me, he is very passionate about improving the lives of destitute and street children.

When I was released from the hospital, my new journey

began in a van which was the CWIN ambulance. They took me to one of the centres, known as the Common Room. It was a rehabilitation centre, as I understood at that time. The Common Room was for all the street children. Whosoever felt that they should be a part of CWIN, they could come there and learn there. It was an innovation to encourage street children and tell them that they can change their lives if they really want to. It would enticing them towards a good life rather than street life. CWIN also had three others transitory rehabilitation centres, one for children below 14 years, these children were kept in the Transitory Rehabilitation Centre A. Teenagers above 14 and up to 18 years were kept in the Transitory Rehabilitation Centre B. There was another centre especially for the girl children.

The Common Room's doors were open to any and all sorts of street children. It was like their home, without any restriction on coming in or going out. Once a child got used to the security of the Common Room, slowly and very gradually, CWIN would put little restrictions on them. Like if you want to sleep in the Common Room, you have to come early in the night and if you want to have lunch and dinner, you have to draw some pictures in the day time. The NGO was generating some interest about normal life of a normal child among street children. For me, it was an orphanage because I could see that mostly orphans only stayed there with me. But the CWIN staff and volunteers would try very hard to not give such a feeling to the children. That's why maybe, they called the shelter a 'Home' or transitory rehabilitation centre. I understood that these shelters were transitory because there used to be some home runners also. CWIN would not keep such children who had parents and homes, in the shelters for long. They felt, if the child had a family, he/she would be much more happier with the family rather than any sort of children's home. But for me, this place was an 'orphanage' because I was an orphan and it was my home.

I couldn't believe that I had a new home to stay in and as I took the first step inside the orphanage gate, I could see a really different world of children. Kids, my age, were all playing in the field. Some staff members were talking to several foreigners and the children were playing with some of them. I could see beautiful elite women were teaching children to play. The kids were not so neat and clean, so I understood that they were no different from me. As I explored around, I could see many toys for the really young children. There were seesaws, slides and swings. Lots of street children were playing and making a noise and I could see staff taking care of these children. I was so confused. I could not figure out where I was. The activist who brought me here from the street introduced me to the other children and the staff of the orphanage. The NGO was quite immense. They had different homes for different categories of children.

Whosoever came straight from the street were first kept in the Common Room.

The Common Room was very good for street children because any time they could get out of there and come back. There was no obligation to stay there because, to deal with street children was no joke since they could turn violent easily if someone tried to compel them. The activists tried hard to teach them some good manners and etiquette. But for street children, whatever they heard from activists, they would get bored of. The people working with the NGO were also very smart. They had a bagful of tricks too to retain the children in the Common Room. Whoever stayed, and learnt drawing and sketches, would get food three times a day. Breakfast, lunch and dinner, but for that, we had to draw at least four cards.

Some children liked it and some didn't like it, but I was among those who liked to learn to draw, rather than get out of there. I was calm and introvert. I didn't want to speak with any child of the orphanage. When other children were playing and loitering around, I would occupy one corner of the Common Room and sit down. The staff of the NGO were very polite, passive and friendly actually. They never beat and hit the children, as street children were very dangerous. If the staff hit or abused them, they could do anything since they were from the street and to survive on the street, they had only learnt how to use violence to defend themselves. One day, when I was sitting leaning against my corner wall, one Miss came to me and asked me, 'Hi! What are you doing here all alone? You don't like to play with other children?' I swung my head towards her and replied, 'You know Miss, I want to be something in my life but I don't know what I should do to be a rich and famous person. Could you please show me the way? And I don't want to go from this place. I want to study because I have heard that this place is the place where children can achieve their dreams.'

When she heard these sentences from me, she just stared at me, smiled and had a puzzled look on her face. Perhaps she was thinking of something but couldn't explain what she was thinking. So I asked her, 'What happened Miss?' She patted my back and said, 'You know, I meet lots of children here but I never found or heard anyone with such deep feelings. This is the first time in my entire career that I met a boy like you and you are such a small child. You are a child with such deep thinking. To do something in life and have ambitions...I really like it and today I am telling you from the core of my heart, that one day you will be a famous and rich person.' One day. It is my belief. When she told me this, I felt empowered and got lots of courage because it was the first time that somebody believed in me, the way I believed in myself.

After a few days, all the staff members at the NGO began to speak to me and began to become my friends.

Gradually, I began to take part in all the activities and get involved in and participate in the different activities. The NGO watched me for a few months. The staff found that I was a child from the street but I was a child without any addiction in terms of drugs and drink. I had no addiction to alcohol or opium, cannabis and hemp. I was totally far from these things, unlike many other street children they brought to the orphanage.

After a few months, the NGO decided to send me from the Common Room facility to their transitory rehabilitation centre where other street children were studying. When I got into that rehabilitation centre, I could see the children were well-dressed and with more toys than at the earlier Common Room. I felt the atmosphere was nicer than the earlier home. I knew the staff members here, rather than the children. Staff members would speak to me and I would talk to them. But the problem was, whenever I approached the other children, I couldn't speak even a single word to them.

ഇൻരാഇൻരാ

The Killer Instinct

After one week at the rehab centre, one teacher came to me while I was playing. I was sliding up and down a slide. He called me, 'Hey! Lad, you come here...' I looked at him. Then, gradually, I moved towards him and said, 'Yes! Sir.' He was standing and resting his right hand on the other slide. I moved close to him. He asked, 'Yes! What's your name?' I answered him very calmly and in a very low voice. I was always afraid someone would ask me to leave. Then he asked me, 'Where is your home?'

Again I replied to him in a very low voice and said, 'Sir, I don't remember my home. I left my home when I was pretty small.' He nodded and asked, 'Okay, then tell me what are your mom and dad's names?' I answered, 'I don't know, Sir. My mom left me when I was six months old. And my dad died when I was just four years old.' For some reason, this person thought I was lying. So he tried to be strict and said, 'You bloody boy. Don't dare to lie to me. C'mon. Tell me the truth!' Then he pushed me. I staggered and stumbled, then fell down on my face. Unfortunately, I banged my head so badly on the slide that the inner side of my lips got cut and my mouth filled with blood. I was fuming. On retrospection, perhaps he had not intended to be so forceful. But I had fallen and hurt myself. I spat out blood on the man's face. He hit out at me and slapped me. It was so hard a slap that tears rolled down from my eyes. Then I started to abuse him rapidly. I looked around desperately to find something, anything I could use as a weapon against him. I found a brick. I then picked up the brick in my hand and smashed it on his head. His head bust. Blood spurted out. I picked up a second brick and smashed that on his face. This time, I missed my target and it struck his back as he had turned away to protect himself. He then ran away... Yet, again, for a third time, I picked up the brick and began to run after him. The man got into the office room and locked himself in. I just sat down at the door and kept abusing him in the filthiest language possible. He phoned other teachers. The staff then put a ladder to an window, got the man out and rushed him to hospital. I did not know this. I continued to sit at the door of the room, to kill him, the moment he ventured out. I sat there till the evening, but he didn't open the door. The brick was in my hand, so nobody dared to come close to me. I did not eat anything all day. My only thought was how to take revenge on the filthy man who had hit me.

Suddenly, I went to sleep at the same door. I remained there for the whole night. In the middle of the night, someone came to me and took the brick from my hand. Next day, when I got up, I felt very hungry. Before I could decide on what to do, I heard a voice, which was growling and growing louder by the minute, as if someone was very angry. This voice said, 'Where is that lad?' After a few minutes, I heard the clattering sound of shoes climbing down the stairs. One big hunk of a teacher soon appeared. He came close to me and said, 'Hey! You come here.' He took hold of my right arm and pulled me up, then dragged me to the play ground.

I bit his hand. He started to kick and punch me. I again started to abuse him. The man was stronger than me and he kept beating and hitting at me and slapping me. I was beyond pain and fear. I began to laugh and laugh. And I continued to abuse him and said, 'If you are a real man, kill me bastard!' Instead of crying, I laughed again and again. At the same time, I was bleeding very badly. But I kept laughing. And said, 'If you are not an eunuch, have the guts to kill me. You sissy man.' And I laughed over and over again. That teacher got tired of beating me. Several times, he flung me far, against the wall. I crashed into the wall and fell. Every time I picked myself up. And every time I laughed. I continued to laugh over and over again and said, 'If you leave me alive, I will kill you, son of a gun.' By this time, the man was really spooked. My laughter, with my mouth full of blood, my battered face and the blood trickling from my nose and the cuts on my head, and even then I was laughing and abusing him. He was scared and quickly scurried away to the office. I couldn't walk but I slowly crawled. All the children around me looked at me with frightened eyes. I must have looked frightful. Soon I reached the office and I shouted loudly, 'Hey! You ba...d. Come on. Kill me.' All the lady staff members were terribly frightened. They started to scream. I crawled up to the man who had hit me. He was cowering. I caught his leg and bit him. He started to scream and jerked his leg away from my mouth. He then ran out of the NGO office and fled. I was still laughing and abusing him.

With all this exertion, I somehow fainted. Once I was unconscious, they took me to the hospital. In the hospital, everything was hunky-dory. I was treated well. The staff thought that I might be a mad boy but the doctors said, 'No. He is absolutely normal. But, maybe, he had some psychological problem.' So, when I had recovered, the NGO caretakers took me back to the transitory rehabilitation centre. This time, when I reached there, no one spoke to me. Everyone had been scared off by my violence.

After being left to myself for a while, a mature voice spoke to me from behind me. 'Hello! My friend, how are you?' When I turned my head, I saw that there were two new staff members. The one who had spoken to me was a total stranger. Yet, at least someone was speaking to me. I replied, 'I am perfect. But I'm going to kill someone and I will have my vengeance.' These people did not seem scared. They smiled and offered me chocolate. Now I gave them an innocent and lovely smile and took the chocolates from their hands. They also smiled and hugged me. I felt so nice. One lady kissed me and I felt so good. So good that somebody was here to love me too.

They stayed at the NGO home for one week and became very good friends. I shared with them the details of each and every moment of my past life, all that I could remember. They also shared with me their love stories, told me about their bad and happy moments. But this was a brief respite. After a week, these new people were gone and I became alone again. Later on I got to know that they were psychologists, and I was their subject of study. They were reading and mapping my behaviour thoroughly, to recommend future action to the NGO. They were not my friends. They were just doing their job. Soon they handed over my report to that centre, and told them why I was so violent. They also recommended, 'Please don't ever beat this boy. Otherwise, he will again turn violent.' They said, 'Always give him love.

Give him love as much as possible. His weakness is chocolate. Whenever he turns violent, offer him a chocolate. He will calm down.'

After passing three months under watch, I was deemed mentally healthy and started to play with other children. They all became my very good friends. CWIN staff were also very kind to me. They admired me, taught me right from wrong, gave me love and care.

One day, a new volunteer teacher came to our home. She was doing MSW (master of social work) and she came as a volunteer and started to teach us English. But she was not my friend. When she was teaching us English one day, all the children were studying and reciting alphabets from the black board. That day I was quiet. I didn't recite anything. So she came to me and said, 'Hi! Why are you not reciting these alphabets?' I didn't say anything. I just remained quiet. Then she hit me on my head with the duster. I didn't say anything to her. I just got up from that class room and fetched a knife from the kitchen. Then I ran straight at her, charging, to shove the knife into her stomach. Fortunately, she moved slightly to the right side, away from my knife. The knife broke the glass of the dolls' shelf behind her and stabbed the belly of the teddy bear, which was inside the shelf. The teacher screamed and immediately ran from the class and started her scooter, parked nearby.

The watchman was asking her, 'What happened, Miss?'

She was so frightened that she did not answer him. She just screamed at him, 'You just shut up and open the door. C'mon faster!' And fled from the premises of the Home.

The watchman saw the knife in my hand and he immediately called the manager of the Home on the intercom. The man came and asked, 'What happened? Why are you making so much noise here?' My hand was bleeding. I had cut my hand with the shelf's broken glass. The Manager asked me, 'What happened? And why is your hand bleeding?' I just turned my head towards him and stared at him. Then he saw the knife in my hand and said, 'You are getting hurt dear. Come on, you need some first aid. Then I will give you chocolate, okay?' Then he walked towards me carefully and took the knife from my hand and said, 'Come on dear.' He took me to the office and cleaned my blood with some antiseptic. Then he gave me some chocolate. I again smiled and went back to the class room. Brand new happiness... as if nothing had ever happened. The Manager called the volunteer and asked, 'What happened?' That volunteer was very frightened. She complained about the carelessness of the manager, because she was totally new and didn't have any knowledge about street children. She said, 'I would have lost my life today and you are responsible for that.'

That Miss never came back to teach us again, but the Manager got into a lot of trouble. He was not able to handle the children in the non-formal education classes, which used to be held daily. For a week he took these informal classes and taught us several games. We learnt to play football but unfortunately, whenever I used to kick the ball towards the goalkeeper, I would miss the target and the ball would land in the neighbour's yard and break the windowpanes. However, other children would shout, 'Wow! What a shot!' But the neighbour's lady wouldn't let us play like that. She would scream and curse us and say, 'Oh, My God! Again my windowpane is gone. Who the hell was that?' Then she would peep through the broken window and shout at us, 'You scoundrels...Wait there, I'll see you all today. Every day, you rascals break my windowpane. Who the hell is going to pay for it?' But most of the time, she would come to our Home and complain to the Manager. She would say, 'Look at my house, and the rest of other neighbours' as well. You will find most of the houses with broken windowpanes. And now the situation is critical, because all the dust and the wind come into the house directly. So, what is the use of fixing windowpanes again and again?' Neighbours used to get totally frustrated with us, but most of the neighbours were also sympathetic, so they wouldn't say anything much.

But sometimes, even our sweet Manager used to get very angry and ban our food. He would tell us, 'First you have to tell the name of the person whosoever has broken the neighbour's windowpane. Then only I will give you the food, alright?' However, the children in that home had love and cared for each other. They were ready to starve, rather than tell the name of the offender to the Manager. Most of the time, I used to break the windowpane. Many a times, the Manager banned our meal but no one ever mentioned my name. Days were happy and in my young life, for the first time there was some enlightenment, new experiences, new people and lessons that added value.

Day by day, I was also becoming nice. All the teachers started to adore and admire me. I used to participate in a variety of activities, especially in social events. Whatever activity I used to get involved in, I used to be always in the limelight and emerged as a leader. This surprised not only my teachers but also me. Some teacher used to say, 'This boy is a diamond. It doesn't matter where he comes from, and where he will go. But he will always shine and be visible from infinite miles away. He just needs to get polished as much as possible, so that he will glitter more effectively and persistently...' This sort of admiration gave me courage. Some of the teachers used to say, 'That adage is true: that whenever you want diamond, you need to go to the coal mine. This boy is also very worthy because whenever he meets people, people do not forget him, everyone loves him and whatever he does, he shines.'

It was an extremely nice sensation because, once upon a time, I was so bad that people used to be scared of me. But gradually, time changed and people started to love me rather than hate me or be frightened of me. It was a divine feeling which came inside me. Teachers used to be very surprised because I used to go to schools and colleges to meet with principals to fix up our programmes and events for sensitising people and to make them aware about the harmful effect of child labour. Everyone started to recognise me in radio channels and some television channels. I could give speeches on different platforms, because I could speak English, Hindi and Nepali but I couldn't read or write it. Whenever I used to meet with other college and school children, they would ask me about my qualifications. When I told them that I had been a street child who had been rescued, my reality would shock people. I never missed the daily informal classes at the orphanage and I was really fond of different books. I couldn't read yet, but I liked to keep them. I hoped to be able to read those books one day. I couldn't imagine that I would go to school in this life because it was really impossible for me to be like a normal regular kid. I was happy to get lodging and getting fed by this centre and somewhere, I was very touched by the compliments of the staff because they used to make me feel alive and gave importance to my existence.

ೲಐೲಐ

My Puppy Love Story

*A*s we know very well, childhood is the most beautiful phase in our life. We are very mischievous and do lots of logical and illogical things in our life. Whosoever really understands children would understand the naughty and beautiful acts of children, and at the same time try to mould them tenderly into good human beings. They wouldn't let the children know that they are being directed to the right track. That intelligent person mentoring children is called the adult. We keep nagging children, 'don't do this, don't do that.' I would say, childhood and 'childlike' is the best part of human life because in that phase we don't ask anyone before doing anything, we just act.

That is called an independent feeling. There is no intension of any conspiracy. Just action. In human lives, childhood is the best phase where a child lives a pure life. He *does things according to his own thoughts. There is a surge within, unobtrusively, to do a certain thing. That's why we like children and we are really lured by their acts of innocence.*

Many adults don't understand children's feelings because they bind themselves with ethics, morals, manners and etiquettes which are completely unnatural and artificial. On the other hand, children's behaviour is natural. An 'imbalance' exists between adults and children. Any working relationship has to work reciprocally. When dealing with children, we should forget about our own concerns. To deal with kids, you need to recall your childhood, then only can you connect with them, like an unbroken mirror. Actually, children are like fragile glasses and the empty black board — it depends on the adults, how they handle or write on them. If you keep nagging, flogging and punishing them instead of loving them, being friendly with them and appreciating their imaginary and real worlds, they will completely break and develop violent psychological behavior. And that would lead to vicious consequences for families and society at large.

In the orphanage home, we had to get up early in the morning and after that, we had to run to freshen up. I was just seven years old at that time. We slept on bunk beds and I used to sleep on the top one. The friend who had the bunk below used to hate it because I was a bed-wetter; in the middle of the night droplets of urine would fall on him. One night, when I was sleeping on the top bunk, I had a dream. All my best dreams were of mustard fields. I was roaming, playing and singing around the mustard field, where lots of butterflies and bees flew around, sucking nectar from the flowers. Some butterflies were sitting on my head, some were sitting on my shoulder. I tried to catch them but could not catch even a single one. Whenever I approached a butterfly and tried to catch it, it would fly away but still I was trying and playing with butterflies and dragonflies... That dream world was very beautiful and pleasing. As I was running to catch those butterflies, I wanted to piddle. I saw a black and giant boulder and then I made up my mind to climb on it.

After struggling for long, I succeeded in reaching the top of that boulder. I hastily unzipped and began to piddle. I felt very calm because I had been struggling so long to pee. A very growling voice from underneath my bed began to shout, 'Hey! You bastard. Come on, get up...' I woke up. Every other child in the dormitory also woke up. Someone lit the light and then all the boys of the dormitory started to asked, 'What happened? Why are you making so much noise in the middle of the night?' That friend, who was sleeping beneath me, replied angrily, 'I am screaming! I'm making noise? You all buggers... Can't you see? He piddled in bed and all the urine sprinkled and came to my mouth while I was asleep. That's why I got up and made so much noise.' When I heard it, I was surprised and then went into denial, 'What! I didn't do anything...' Everyone in that dormitory then started to grin and laughed their guts out. In the meantime, I started to fumble at my pants and I found that they were indeed wet. I then began to plead with my friend to forgive me and said, 'I'm sorry bro... it happened by mistake. I thought I was piddling in the mustard field, I don't know how it fell on your face.'

Then every boy in that room looked at my friend's face and asked, 'Your face is wet with piss. How does it taste?' Then they began to smirk at first, and then to laugh... uncontrollably. Laughter echoed in that dormitory in the middle of the night. My friend ran off to the washroom in the meanwhile, and having washed his face thoroughly, he came back. He did not find it funny. He then went to sleep, warning me, 'Hey! Basu. Now listen to me very carefully. Don't piss again, I am telling you.' I nodded, 'Okay buddy, don't worry. It will not happen again. It's enough.' But the boys of the dormitory kept laughing and provoking him, 'Hey! Ram Kumar... how was the taste?' He didn't reply and slowly, we all went to sleep because we knew very well that early in the morning, we would have to get up.

In the morning, the Warden of the Home came to our dormitory and said, 'Come on, get up kids... you all are still sleeping? Come on, hurry up...' I got up and started to rub my eyes, when one voice came from my side, 'Hey! Basu. Did you again do that?' Once again, everyone started to grin but the Warden got annoyed and said, 'Why are you kids laughing? Come on, get out of this room and freshen up.' After getting ready, we had to go for PT (physical training or exercise). After that, we used to get breakfast and then had to attend our informal classes.

That day, when we reached class, a surprise awaited us. The surprise was our new Ma'am. She was like an Angel, since she was so very beautiful. When she came to our class room along with our Manager, a collective, 'Wow!! Who is she?', came from the children. The Manager said, 'Good morning kids... she is your new madam. Anything more? Okay?' To draw their attention, I just got up and said, 'Alright, Sir...' The Miss asked the Manager, 'Who is this kid? He is very cute.' The Manager replied, 'He is our Hero. Everyone calls him Basu because everyone loves him. And I must tell you, you will also like him very much, very soon.' She smiled and said, 'So impressive!' I just continued to smile and kept looking only at her. It was, however, not just I, there were lots of my friends who too kept smiling and staring at her. One by one, the new teacher made us get up and introduce ourselves. I was just looking at her and smiling within myself. She gave her own introduction and said, 'I do modeling plus social work. I would like to be your friend, alright?' I smiled and said, 'Alright Miss...'

After that, she asked us, 'What would you like to study?' The boys replied, 'Anything...' She thought for a few seconds, 'Hum...Okay. I will teach you English, is that okay for you?' All of us replied, 'Okay Miss...' she wrote A-Z alphabets on the black board and asked us to recite them after her, but I got up and took out the thick English book that I always carried around. The book contained fairy tales and I sat at one corner of the room with it. Miss looked at me and said, 'Hey! Basu, you know English?' I replied, 'Yes I do.' The teacher was surprised and said, 'You are very impressive.' After that, all the boys told her, 'Yes! Miss. He knows very good English. Most of the times it is he who tells us lots of stories through English books.' I was a little scared because I didn't actually know how to read. I used to tell the stories to all of my friends with the help of the pictures which illustrated the story pages. Then, I had plenty of imagination... All fairy tales had the Good battling Evil. I just had to translates what the pictures told me, to all. Ma'am came to me and said, 'Okay Basu. Could you please read some paragraph from this book?' She asked me to do something that I didn't want to do, but I tried to fool her and pretended to read, 'Blah... Blah... Blah...' She spoke in English and said, 'Come on Basu. Don't joke with me. Read properly.'

Then I started to think, 'Hum...I think this Miss knows English.' After that, I asked her in English only, 'Ma'am, you know English?' She said, 'Yes. When I was small, I studied in an English school and when I finished my

schooling, I studied in college. It was also English medium.'
I was blushing very badly and I told her, 'Ma'am, could
you come outside for a minute please?' She asked me in
English, 'Why?' I again pleaded with her, to come outside.
Then she said, 'Okay.' All my friends thought that Basu is
talking in English with the new Ma'am. I got up, and then
got out from the class room. Ma'am came after me and
asked me, 'What happened?' I stammered, 'See Miss... I
don't know English to read and write, but I can speak it.
All my friends respect me very much and I do have pride.
So, please don't let them know that I don't know English
to read! Please...' she smiled and didn't say anything. This
annoyed me, especially as she continued to smile. I then
said, 'If you want to be friends with me, you have to take
care of my prestige, otherwise I will not be friends with
you, in any case.' Then I started to walk away.

She caught my hand and said, 'Okay...Okay...I will
not let anyone know, and I will keep it a top secret. This
is between you and me okay...?' I was very happy to hear
it and said, 'Okay... thank you very much. So... we are
friends?' I asked her and offered her my hand to shake. She
smiled and said, 'Of course, friend.' She also caught my
hand and shook it. I also shook hands with her and said,
'Okay Miss. We are friends, so now you have to take care
of me.' She said, 'Fine, but what would I need to do?' I
demanded, 'See...? You will not say anything to me in the

class room and you will not ask me to study. But when we get a break, you will come to our rose flower garden to teach me to read and write English, alright?'

She said, 'Of course, my Majesty. I will do that. But what I saw is, you get upset very fast. So, you do promise to me, you will control yourself and will not get angry quick? Alright?' I also became very honest in our friendship. I also promised her to not get angry, and said, 'Alright Angel.' She was startled and asked, 'What...?' I again said, 'Angel...' She asked me, 'Why did you say that?' I smiled and replied, 'Ma'am you are very pretty and I would prefer to call you Angel, rather than Ma'am.' She smiled and lifted her right hand to tousle my hair. Then she said, 'You are a real cute lad. I like you very much.' After having a long and friendly conversation, the teacher returned to the class room and started to teach the rest of the children.

After a few minutes, I also returned to the class room and sat at the same corner where I had sat earlier. I then pretended to read the same book, but this time my Angel was looking at me and smiling. After the break, I took Angel to our Home's rose garden and asked her to teach me but on that first day, she wanted to know about me. So she asked me some questions like, 'Where are you from? Where is your Mom and Dad?' When I told her my story, she was shocked and weeping. I could see the tears that rolled down her cheeks. I began to think that, 'She is my real friend, because she understands my feelings so deeply.'

On that first day, Angel asked me one more question. She said, 'How can you speak English?' I answered, 'I don't know how. But when I was small, in the street, since that time I could speak English. You know, once when I was new in the begging job, my friend told me that, if you want to earn more money, you should know English in order to beg from foreigners. So, he started to speak some words of English. Once he spoke out some words in English, I interrupted him and asked him if what he said was English. He said, "Yes." I told him, "I know this language." He was also surprised and asked me, "How come, you understand this!" I had only one answer at that time too. "I don't know how." I tell you too, I don't know how I know English.'

My Angel told me that, 'You know Basu, according to your history, your mom and dad were educated. So they might have been speaking in English with you. That's how you can understand English.' After I had shared my feelings and emotions with her, she told me that, 'You should study very hard Basu, because you have that quality to do something or achieve certain goals.' So, then on, every day we used to meet in the break or recess. She used to teach me to read and write. Gradually our friendship became deep. My friends often saw her on television because she was also a model. Sometimes, they would make lewd comment on her. I got into fights with them over her.

My buddies started to ask me, 'Hey! Basu why you get so tense, whenever we say something about Madam?' Then once, I told them, 'See buddy? You all are my friends, alright?' Everyone nodded their heads. I said then, 'there is no doubt?' After a pause, I told them, 'Angel, who is your Ma'am, she is my girlfriend and I love her very much. So, please don't dare to say anything about her. She is like your sister-in-law. You all got that?' I was just eight-years-old.

All my friends started to laugh at me and said, 'Have you ever thought about her age and yours? You are such a baby in front of her.' One small friend spoke up, 'Have you ever told her that you love her?' I said, 'No. But I love her.' When my friends saw that I was really serious about her, they stopped commenting about her in my presence. Every day, as we gathered on the terrace and spoke and thought about my Angel's wedding, some friend would say, 'Hey! Basu, would you call us if you get married to your Angel?' And some of them would ask me, 'What... gift should we give you?' It became an everyday past-time. You can say, those days were some of the happiest days of my life. But there is a saying that once you become so happy, there will be bad days which will follow. You have to face it calmly. This means, if there is dawn, there is night too. One day, I heard that there would be a farewell ceremony for my Angel. She was going away. I felt very bad. I sat and cried in the same rose garden where she used to teach me to read and write. But that day, she was giving speeches on the stage of our auditorium.

I was just sitting and weeping. My gang of friends couldn't find me in the auditorium. They soon came looking for me in the garden. 'Hey! Basu you are crying here and your girlfriend is about to go.' I looked at them with tearful eyes, then asked, 'What can I do...?' One little six-year-old said, 'Hey! Basu, have you seen movies?' I said, 'Obviously, yes.' Then he said, 'See...? In the movies, once the hero proposes to the heroin, they stay together. So, if you want to make her stay here, you need to propose to her.' All the friends said, 'Yes. He is right...come on Basu, you need to propose to her.' But the strange thing was, I didn't know how to propose to her. Once again, my small friend gave me the idea and said, 'See...? Pluck one rose from here and directly go on the stage and kneel down. Then offer her the rose and then ask her, would she be yours?' I plucked the rose as my friend had said then walked down toward the auditorium.

When I reached near the stage, I was still crying. Once my Angel saw me crying, she asked me to come up on the stage. My friends were behind me and encouraging me. Once I got on the stage, I said to Madam, 'Dear Ma'am. I want to say something to you.' She asked me, 'What do you want to say?' My friends again encouraged me and said, 'Come on, say it.' I was still weeping. Even then, I got close to her and kneeled down, then offered her the rose and said in stammering voice, 'Ma'am, I love you very much and I want to marry you.' Suddenly, my friends also started to weep and said, 'Yes Ma'am. Basu loves you. Ever since you came here, to our Home, he loves you very much.' All the teachers looked very shocked. One of the male teachers came to me and said, 'You wait, what a boy is this, who doesn't have any respect for the teacher.' He tried to move me away from the stage. But my Angel began to cry and replied, 'Of course, I love you too and I would marry you also. But now, you are very small. You just reach my waist. When you become as big as I am, then I will marry you, alright? Till then you and I are boyfriend and girlfriend. You write me letters, and I will write you letters.' Then she gave me her telephone number and address. After that she gave me a very tight hug and kissed my cheeks. She said, 'whenever you miss me and feel like calling me, just give a buzz, and at whatever time you want to meet me, you just call me, alright?' After that she left with moist eyes.

Later on, we often spoke over the phone. I would write to her too and she too wrote back. This process went on for one year. However, slowly but surely, I understood the reality and found out what was right and what was wrong. Then one day, I went to her home and said, 'Ma'am I understood that we are just friends. I can't be your lover.' She smiled and stretched out both her hands, and she kneeled down and gave me warm hugs and kisses, and said to me, 'I know. You are a very innocent and cute friend and I love your simplicity. If you would have been my age, I would have married you, my sweetheart!' That day, I also met her real boyfriend and had a very pleasing conversation with him too. He was kidding and told me, 'I think I should fight with you, because you are so cute and handsome. I envy you. Even my girlfriend wants to marry you, rather than me.' I took it very seriously and said, 'Okay, you want to fight...alright? Anytime.' He smiled then replied, 'No...No.... You are very brave also. I don't have the guts to fight with you, because you are a genuine lover of my girlfriend.'

I was shy and bowed my head. He laughed at me and said, 'Oh! My God! This brave man is also shy. Come on buddy, don't feel shy.' My Angel made tea and offered her boyfriend, then she also offered a glass of milk to me too. After that, when I was about to leave, she walked with me to her car and told her driver, 'Please drop him till his Home, alright?' The Driver replied, 'Yes Ma'am.' She again kneeled down and hugged me, but I did not still get into the car. I stood outside. She again came to me with tearful eyes and kissed me, then said, 'Okay my sweetheart. Bye. Maybe, we will not meet again, because I am getting married and going to America forever. But I will miss you so much.' It was a very heartbreaking day for me. I had gone to her home that day, because she had called me. She couldn't tell me that she was getting married and going away to America forever earlier. When I was just about to leave, she told me this and ran away into the house. I also got into the car and her boyfriend kept waving his hand through the window and saying, 'Bye.' Her Driver dropped me to my Home, and once I got out of the car, I ran to my dormitory.

I wept for her all evening and didn't eat anything that night. I missed her every day. But gradually, I started to stop thinking about her. Then, when she was finally married, she gave me a buzz from the airport when she was leaving the country. That time too, I cried for her and she also cried over the phone for me. It never rang again but I kept my eyes on the phone every day, for two or three months. However, reality of life caught up with me. I understood, what life was all about. It was about loss and gain.

What I have experienced is: these kind of feelings emerge spontaneously in every child during their growing and developing phase. But we should make sure that we put them on the right track while traveling together on their path, rather than hurt them and break their beautiful and extremely innocent hearts. Whatever they do is pretty much natural and children generally do not have any self interest. You can say, it is a divine act and one of unadulterated simplicity. So the responsibilities of adults are to respect their innocent sentiments and enlighten them with love, as my Angel did for me. If you are a real human being, you can't run from things like this. It is your own self and truth that make you admit to emotions and feelings. If you claim you have succeeded in giving up these things, it means you are not a genuine human being.

ೂୠ୬ୠ

Global March Against Child Labour

It was the morning of 15 January 1998. Someone knocked my door and asked me to come to the lobby. As I got there, an unbelievable sight confronted me. There was a sea of children before me. Some were white and black, and some were Asian. The children were accompanied by their chaperons who were representatives of local organisations that they belonged to. All the children were around 10-15 years old. I was quite astonished to see the children from different countries. For me, it was a beautiful and unseen world. It was like a dream too, and it was one of the most beautiful moments in my life that I was part of that sea of young and vibrant humanity. It wasn't just me who was so surprised. Each and every child present there must have been equally surprised. Everyone was looking at each other and trying to figure out who was who... but suddenly, one man came there who stood out. His face was covered with a beard and he was about six feet tall. He looked like a very simple man. I had heard once that simple living and high thinking should be the goal of a person. As I saw this man, this thought crossed my mind. His name was Kailash Satyarthi.

Satyarthi wished each and everyone and said hello. We too greeted him. I wondered, who was he...? I was just looking at him. I didn't like his beard. He spotted me and said, 'Hey! What's your name?' I answered him in a low voice. He said, 'How old are you?' I said, 'Nine years old.' He was very surprised and said, 'Oh! My God, you are just nine years old? Is there anyone else of this age?' I was scared of him, because he had a beard. Suddenly he hugged me, because I happened to be the youngest 'core marcher' in our team. Then he asked me, 'How are you son?' I smiled and began to talk to him. In a few minutes, we became friends and I was no longer scared of his beard. He made me sit on his lap and gave us an introduction of the movement of the Global March Against Child Labour, for which we had gathered in this Philippino city.

Then Kailashji, who was the founder of Global March Against Child Labour, stood up to address the gathering. He welcomed us and said:

'Dear children, You are the torch-bearers of tomorrow. You have gathered over here to create history with your potential to make this world beautiful for all children. You are the ones with the moral power, high enough to shake mountains, let alone the conscience of global leaders. I have full faith in your power, strength and capabilities. Children, you are the ones that inspired me to walk on a path less travelled, when I completed engineering twenty years ago. I chose to fight against child labour as I have always felt that, it is the worst crime on humanity that ruins childhood.

'Children, you have overcome the most difficult challenges of your life and have emerged victorious as you stand here today. You will become the voice of the children who are still trapped in slavery. I salute you. You are a select few who were chosen by the partner organisations of Global March from across the world. Thank you so much for volunteering to be a part of this big battle against child labour — a journey that would become one of our most memorable experiences hereafter. Million of tender children like you have fallen prey to child labour. They are made to work day and night. They do not get to meet their parents. They get very little to eat. Sometimes they go to bed hungry. They do not get money for the work they do. These children are not allowed to play and enjoy. They cannot attend school like other children. They are often beaten up by their masters for small mistakes. All of you come from different parts of the globe. You have faced similar hardships in your lives, but you are the only ones who have the survival instinct and the unrelenting desire to do whatever it takes to save millions of children who are stuck in child labour and exploitation.

'Those children look at us with big hope and great expectations and we will not disappoint them. It is the right of all children to get a dignified life like any other citizen. Together we are fighting against those who steal this right from innocent children like you. I know that you are the loudest voice against child labour and exploitation. This is your opportunity to be heard by the policy makers of this world. I know that when all of you will speak, the entire world will listen. My partners, volunteers and I are there to guide you at every step of this first ever global fight against child labour, where you as survivors of the suffering have chosen to transform your pain into your biggest strength. You are the real change makers.

'Today will always be remembered in the fight against child labour. You all are the part of the inaugural leg of "Global March Against Child Labour" here in Manila that will travel all over the world in the coming months. There would be two more legs that are being simultaneously flagged off from Sao Paulo in Brazil and Cape Town in South Africa. Over the next six months, together we will travel around 80,000 kilometers which is more than twice the circumference of earth. It is nothing short of a magic that you will discover for yourself in the days that follow. There will be a lot of interaction as we move from here. You will get to meet so many children who will share their experience with you. We will cross countries, cities, towns, districts and villages in demand for a strong international law against the worst forms of child labour. You will meet people of different nationalities, backgrounds, ethnicities, abilities etc. and you will be able to see for yourself how quickly we multiply and the chorus against child labour gets louder. As we move ahead, you will get to know about the universal rights of children and the way to realize them. I am sure you will get to make friends for a life time during this march.

'The adult representatives of the Global March and partner organisations will answer all your queries, so please do not hesitate to ask questions and I assure you that you will be answered and everything explained systematically. If you are still not satisfied by the answer, I am available round the clock to address your concerns.

'So, my dear young friends, It is a fight by the children for the children. It is the power of unity. It will be the biggest show of solidarity for the children who are languishing in dark corners of the world. This is the time to work for them so that in future, children don't have to suffer the way you did.'

Kailashji's electrifying speech left us spell-bound. We immediately fell in love with him. A new family had just been created and we could feel the hero inside us.

As I heard these introductory speeches, I was fired with great zeal. I started to think about the march. I had gone through the pain of earning a living as a child worker. I was so right and ready for such a campaign. I really liked Kailashji, because he was working for children who wouldn't even dare to dream to live a life. He had also called me 'son'. After that, I just tagged along with only him... Somehow, he was also really fascinated by me. When we broke after the activity, we went to the cafeteria and had breakfast. It was great for me. I could see a variety of dishes, so immediately I ordered roasted chicken and my mouth began to drool as I sat at the table and started to eat the chicken. I remembered the worst day in my life and returned to the flashback.

ഇൻ§ഇൻ§

Kids' Army Marching

While thinking about my painful past, that morning in Manila, I ate at the cafeteria and looked around, thinking what a beautiful morning it was.

I had never dreamt of such a morning. This was the dawn of my brand new life. It was the morning of the Global March Against Child Labour.

I was the child who was very active in promoting the cause of child workers in Nepal. Activists of CWIN loved me a lot because now, I was no longer an aggressive and violent street child. I was the child who was talking about 'philosophy of life', helping newcomers to CWIN shelters to think about life. At the same time, as I was helping the organisation with other street children. I was also going to various leadership training workshops. The first training I got was in a Child Rights course and workshop conducted by Redd Barna. I remember this leadership training programme as this was the first one that I ever participated in, and it was on children's rights. I never knew that children had so many rights! In that workshop there were lots of children from all around, and from several NGOs active in this sector in Nepal. At the end of the workshop, I was chosen the 'leader' in that workshop and everybody appreciated my talk and the views I expressed about the problems of street children. After that, I became very famous in CWIN. CWIN hosted South Asia's Regional Secretariat for Global March Against Child Labour. Sir Gauri Pradhan was one of the co-founders of South Asian Coalition on Child Servitude (SACCS) with Kailashji and his dear friend since 1988. Sir Gauri was already my friend, but now he became a fan. He understood that I had the 'inbuilt talent' as a child, something he had been talking about for years. He had advocated the 'telling of the true story' of a destitute child to explain to people what exactly a child worker went through on the streets, in homes and commercial establishments.

After sometime, there was talk of CWIN participating in an international programme to send children from Nepal to campaign against child labour across the world. The organisers were searching for children who had been survivors of exploitation themselves and had the potential to emphatically voice their concerns to international policy makers. They were conducting lots of interviews with children who had been child labourers. Soon some CWIN teachers came to me and began to talk to me, from the perspective of a potential campaigner. I passed the organisation's benchmark and they thought I was the best guy to participate in a worldwide campaign called the 'Global March' against child labour. After the first round of interviews, a senior activist, Tarak Dhital spoke to me. I think it was for the second time that I had met him. He was very casual, however. He said, 'Hey! Basu, I have heard a lot about you.' He then had a long chat with me. After passing his scrutiny, I was finally sent to Sir Gauri, at the head office of CWIN.

As I went up to the reception, the receptionist asked me to sit. Then Sir Gauri called me into his office. He asked me to take a seat. I was a little nervous this time because I knew that he was taking my interview to select the child campaigner for the international campaign. I sat down on the chair and he asked me, 'How are you?' I replied with a smile, 'Good, Sir.'

He said, 'You know why we are here, right?'

I replied, 'Yes Sir. Children all around the world have lots of problems. Now you are going to select who can be the child representative from Nepal for millions of children who are still in slavery, orphan children who are living on the streets.'

He smiled and replied, 'Well that's pretty much true... So, tell me why you should be chosen for this?'

I answered, 'Sir, I don't really know if I should be chosen for this or not. Only one thing I have in my mind, that if I can go there, I have plenty of questions for those governments and I want to share my story with the whole world. I want to ask why millions of children have to spend their lives on the street. I have heard that governments are responsible for taking care of us. Why then do millions of children die on the streets in every part of the world? I think I should be chosen because I have seen life so closely on the street. I have seen children dying on the street and becoming orphans on the street.' Sir knew that I talked very intensely and he already knew of my concern about orphaned and abandoned children.

So he said, 'Well... you are very small but you are the perfect boy to be one of the child participants at the Global March Against Child Labour. Wish you all the best!' I smiled and was very happy because I knew how important this Global March was, because I had been told by many staff members at CWIN about the scale and magnitude of this event. I was lucky to be one of the children from Nepal chosen for this march and I was very thrilled. I got up and said, 'Sir, as far as I know, it is the children, the victims themselves, who are going to write this history?'

He said, 'Let's hope. I wish children will make people

across the world aware about their problems and that's why I have chosen you. You have leadership skills, my friend and I am sure you'll not let us down.'

I replied, 'No Sir. I'll not.' Then I got out of the office and started to imagine how I would go. Would I fly in an airplane or travel by a bus? And many more things were on my mind. All the staff, and the teachers and, of course, my friends were happy for me. I had now become CWIN's champion. I was also informed by Sir Gauri that another child from CWIN, Vishnu, had also been selected for the March.

This is how, now I was in a Manila hotel this fine morning.

After our breakfast, we gathered at the lobby. This was different. True, all of us were children. But we were children with a lot of pain in our hearts. Each one of us in that lobby had come from different corners of the world. Each one of us had been a working child. Each one of us had a story to tell. Each one who had gathered in this lobby with the desire to create history had been a child labourer. So I could understand the pain of these children swarming all around me. The people and the children gathered here did not know each other's languages. I could see the small tiny hands making gestures to explain their feelings. However, we soon got to know one another through our songs, our skits, role plays, poems and slogans on child labour and as we shared our personal stories, stories of intolerable pain, our bonding was further cemented. This sharing and telling made us one. It was like unity in diversity. That's how we understood the word 'solidarity' and started to write slogans like, 'Go Go Global March... Stop... Stop... Child labour... We want education... No more tools in tiny hands... We want books and we want toys...' Global March partners, volunteers and staff ensured that we were at complete ease. All of us were insured for any unforeseen incident. The objective of each and every activity that had been planned well in advance, was explained to us. This made the going smooth.

In just one day, we became close to one another through a series of activities. We did not know about languages and cultures and we were not aware of discriminations of colour, race, religion and creed. Here we belonged to one religion. It was humanity. And we didn't have any particular country, because we children were the army of the Global March Against Child Labour under the leadership of Kailash Satyarthi. We were full of enthusiasm, potential and with fire in our hearts. We wanted to bring justice for children from every corner of the world. We were known as 'core marchers' and I was the youngest core marcher. Finally, after a long preparation, we started the March from Manila, the capital of the Philippines. We shouted slogans and walked the roads, chanting. I was really excited at the idea of raising slogans. Thousands of other children from the schools and shelter homes joined us in solidarity besides teachers, social workers, trade union members etc. I held the megaphone, then started to lead the sloganeering. In a powerful voice, I said, 'Go... Go...' and the rest of the others would shout in a loud voice and said, 'Global March... Stop... Stop... Child Labour. We want... Education. No more tools in tiny hands... We want books and we want toys. These slogans were created after meticulous discussions that Global March had held with its partner organisations across the globe in consultation with the children that were at the heart of this unparalleled march.' The whole city resonated with our slogans. The electronic media did not rest, they clicked hundreds of pictures of the march and the core marchers. Soon we reached the Parliament House in Manila. The people there welcomed us like VIPs.

As we entered the Parliament House, I started to peer around. I could see lots of guards with machine guns hanging on their shoulders. We core marchers were asked to sit on a row of chairs. Then we started to raise slogans and the former President, Cory Aquino and other leaders came and sat with us. After that, Kailashji had an half-an-hour discussion with them regarding the problems of child labour. They were not really aware of the seriousness of the issue of child labour in their country. Some core marchers and local children from the Philippines told them their stories of hardship.

After listening to all the speakers, the political leaders

promised us that they would work towards eradication of child labour. Admiring the courage of the core marcher children, they said, that they were very happy that children who had gone through the pain of being child labours themselves were fighting for the rights of other children. Children are demanding their rights and walking through the city streets to make a bright future for the world. They further said that they would pray for all the children. They wished us luck. When we heard this from the leadership, we were very happy and applauded them. Then they hugged us, even me and shook hands with the marchers. We then returned to the hotel where we stayed. That day, we were all very tired and excited and we were thankful for the rest.

Next morning, when I got up, my facilitator came towards me with the newspaper in his hand. He smiled and gave me the newspaper. When I saw it, I was just stunned. 'Oh! My God! I can't believe this. Uh, I... never ever thought in my life that one day I would appear in the newspaper and ah... my picture would get printed on the front page in large size. Thank God for such a wonderful moment.' I was very happy to just see my picture appear in the newspaper. I felt that, 'Now I'm not just a street child. I am happy. I am becoming famous. I am loved and respected. I am an important child for all the people here.' So, with this feeling and with gladness, I went to the cafeteria. When I reached there, I could see the news on television and my own self with the rest of the other children. We were elated and were cheering in excitement.

From Philippines we marched through Vietnam, Cambodia, Thailand, Malaysia, Bangladesh, Nepal, India, Pakistan, Iran, Turkey, Greece, Italy and Switzerland etc. Every day during the march we walked through streets, pavements and neighborhoods in cities, towns, districts, villages. While marching we held placards and banners and shouted slogans on the top of our voice. We used to be accompanied by drummers, band players etc. for drawing public attention.

At least five-six public meetings, street theatre, corner meetings, rallies were a regular affair every day during the Global March. While marching, thousands of local supporters of Global March used to hop on and start marching with us in the huge caravan, wherever we went.

Marching all across gave me a lot of knowledge about child labour, people, various problems, different cultures, costumes and outlook. Rather than the differences, I found something very common and similar in the whole world. These were emotions, love and humanity. This is precisely what Global March had endeavored. We usually divide ourselves country-wise, religion-wise, and on the basis of race and castes. But here I stood under the umbrella of the Global March Against Child Labour with all the others, hailing only one religion, ie. religion of love and humanity. These are natural, gifted by God but the rest are manmade, which separate people and take them away from love and humanity. They forget that they are nature's beings and start indulging in wars. So what I really learnt is that I should not have any man-made religion. I always follow the path of love and humanity because above everything else I am a human being. There is just one God. People worship God in different forms and that's the real cause of emerging different religions. So, rather than fighting for religion, we should follow only one religion — that of humanity since it teaches us just love. Because that is what we really crave for.

As I kept traveling from one country to another, I became famous and people started calling the core marchers, heroes. I used to be extremely busy and surrounded by a lot of electronic media. Global March had made elaborate preparations to ensure that children and other core marchers like me are not heckled by media and journalists. Every radio, television and newspaper wanted to talk to me and the other core marchers. Organisers of the Global March had meticulously planned the programme, so that every child core marcher got a chance to present her/his case in the media interviews and on speaking platforms. The media focus increased to such an extent that even when we were sitting and eating, they would ask for interviews. People would click so many pictures of us at every step, it was nothing short of VIP treatment. I would say it was no less than the experience of being a famous Hollywood star. However, soon I had tired of the attention and ran, when I spotted a camera.

I never ever understood time. Because when times change, life gains a lot of unexpected experiences, as happened in my life. There was a time when I was on the street where people used to hate me. Now people wanted to talk to me and they loved me. Global March had come as an instrument of metamorphosis in the lives of all of us core marchers. The strangest thing was that people wanted to learn lots of thing from us. With every change in my life, I realised that I had to remain prepared both for the worst as well as the best.

Our movement was growing and eradication of child labour from the world appeared an achievable goal. The core marchers were never tired of raising a slogan for children's rights. They used to shout as much as they could, and thus, shouting slogans and chanting on the roads, we reached Rome, the capital of Italy, one day. We travelled in a very comfortable and luxurious bus. As the bus started to move, we could see many beautiful things all around. Buildings, fountains, gardens. Suddenly I saw a boy and a girl smooching at the bus stand. At that sight, every core marcher's eyes popped out. I was known as the Little Master and I was very mischievous. I shouted at the couple, 'Carry on you sexy guys.' Then the whole team started to laugh. We just laughed and laughed all the way. My facilitator came to me and asked me, 'What were you looking at outside and laughing at?' I immediately became quiet and said, 'No, I am not laughing here. But the rest of them are laughing. I am just looking at the beautiful scenario and enjoying it. Oh! Look at that Sir, what a beautiful building, isn't it?' My facilitator looked at me and said, 'Every building, statue and lane is beautiful here in Rome. So have a look and enjoy it.' After that, my facilitator moved on to his seat. After a while, we reached the guest house where we were supposed to stay. We all got off the bus and moved to the reception to get our room numbers. When we got the room numbers, we came to collect our luggage. What I saw was a huge guy named Alam Rahaman, who was lifting at least fifteen bags, hanging them all around his body and staggering towards the reception. He had my bags too, so I ran towards him and said, 'Dear Bro, give it to me. I'll help you.' He chuckled and said, 'No, No.... Don't worry. I'll do it. Come to the reception.' Then he staggered... finally he threw the bags on the floor upon reaching the reception.

To tell you briefly about Alam Rehman. This Canadian is a very intelligent, hardworking and committed man. He had visited India in 1996 and had been with Kailashji when he was conceptualising the Global March Against Child Labour. Alam had participated in some activities with Kailashji at his Indian organisation, the Bachpan Bachao Andolan and soon became an inextricable part of the team in the run up to the Global March. He was Kailashji's right hand in the execution of Global March. I first met him in Bangkok and drew a lot of inspiration from him. Among the very important motivators of the Global March movement, Alam liked to be like a child with children, because he loved children. Alam became a very close friend during the Global March.

En-route, the local organisers of the Global March had also scheduled a special programme in the holy Vatican City. Pope John Paul II had sent his blessings to the Global March and had also hailed a special sermon for its success.

The next day was a very big day for the core marchers because we had a meeting with the Mayor of the city of Rome. I was elected among the team members to speak about the Global March and the harmful effect of child labour on the stage. The other core marchers sat with the audience. I was with the VIPs on the stage. When I took my seat, there was a girl called Martina who sat next to me. She was a very pretty girl around my age. She was working for the child rights forum and fighting for child rights. When the anchor called her name, she made a speech on the importance of child rights and what really her child right forum was doing for children. When she finished her speech, I told her, 'Hi! It was really a beautiful speech.' she smiled and replied, 'Thank you very much.' After her turn, my name was called. So I pulled the microphone and began to speak on child labour and the Global March. When I finished, everyone clapped very enthusiastically. When I took my seat, Martina asked me, 'What is your name?' I could not understand what she said, so I asked the interpreter to translate it, and replied, 'Oh! Sorry. I can't speak Italian well. My name is Basu Rai.' Then she smiled and looked at me and said, 'Okay.'

After that, I too smiled at her. Speeches were going on in the hall. I was listening keenly to all the speeches. She gave me a piece of paper but my facilitator was sitting by my left side. So he took the paper and read it. After a while, he said, 'Hey! This girl wants to make friends with you. Wow! It's great!' I replied to the facilitator, 'So, what should I say to her?' He replied, 'Whatever she says, just say yes, yes. That's it.' I responded to him and said, 'Alright.' I turned towards her and said, 'Yes.' She smiled and caught my hand. As she caught my hand... the meeting was over and everyone began to move out to the park. She asked me, 'Hey! You are so cute... I like you, would you be my boyfriend?' I immediately said, 'Obviously.' She had caught my hand while we were getting out of the hall. She kissed me in the park. Some core marchers saw us and exclaimed, 'Oh! My God... look at them!' It was very embarrassing for me because a girl was kissing me. I had not yet figured out what was really going on with me. So, here I was with a girlfriend I had found within an hour of meeting her. Much later I realised I was the boyfriend of the Mayor's daughter. Suddenly someone came to call her, so she got into the car and said, 'Bye', then moved on. We also had to walk towards the bus. As I got into the bus, everyone started to make fun of me and asked me, 'Hey! How was the kiss?' I was shy and couldn't reply. Suddenly one facilitator from Indonesia asked me, 'Did you take her address and phone number?' I was shocked when she asked me this question. I immediately replied, 'No! No...! I... uh... I didn't take the addresses and phone number.' She exclaimed, 'What? Are you saying that you forgot to take her address? Oh! My God, what a guy you are.' Everyone felt sad for me because they were all so happy that I had found a pretty gorgeous girlfriend.

So when we reached our accommodation, I caught the hand of Maria Rosa, who was representing MANITESE in the capacity of the National Coordinator of Global March in Italy and asked her, 'Could you please get me the address of the girl Martina, who was sitting beside me?' She said, 'Well... I don't think I can, but I'll try.' I was happy. In the end, however, Maria Rosa could not find her address. I was sad but it was our last day in Italy and I couldn't sleep all night. Next morning, while we were having breakfast everyone kept asking me, 'Hey! Basu, what happened to you? You seem to be very sad and blue today.' I answered, 'Nothing... happened.' One facilitator from Nepal, her name was Kabita, spoke up and said, 'Well... he must be thinking about the girl who kissed him yesterday.' All the other core marchers laughed loudly at that.

After finishing breakfast, everyone got back to the rooms and started packing their luggage. I also went to my room and packed up. We scrambled towards the bus and stuffed our bags into the hold. The core marchers were all crowding around when the facilitators started to say, 'come on children, hurry up. Please get into the bus quickly because we need to reach the harbour as soon as possible. Come on...' Within a single minute, every core marcher got into the bus and was ready to go. When the bus started to move, tears began to roll down my eyes. I was crying alone. Unexpectedly, one woman facilitator saw me crying all alone, she immediately rushed towards me, then she held and hugged me very tightly and said, 'Why are you crying? Are you crying for that girl?'

I said, 'Yes.' She said, 'Okay.... alright.... And now listen to me very carefully. You know, this is called life. Everyone here in this world is not forever and everyone has to depart from a certain point, time and place. As you can see, today we all core marchers are together. Let me tell you that, the day is not long when everyone will have to go back to their own destinations. So don't cry for her. Well, anyway, she was beautiful wasn't she? How was the kiss?' When she asked me this question, I smiled and felt embarrassed and began to wipe my tears. She then began to tease me and said, 'Come on, look at this boy who is shy and blushing.' Then chuckling and grinning, she began to talk more and we had this long conversation all the way to the harbour. We finally got off the bus and our facilitators began to lead us toward the harbour.

I never thought I would ever cross the sea.

Sometimes life is totally incredible and astonishing, because it gives you such experiences and knowledge that you've never dreamt of. Experiences are very essential because they give you deep and pure knowledge, rather than superficial ones. And I would say, profound knowledge is the perfect knowledge. People who believe in complete knowledge, they go through certain experiences, because there is a vast difference between knowledge and experiences. One can get knowledge from books, hearsay and seeing around but for experiences, one needs to go via certain way where one confronts certain situations and particular things. It is not so easy to travel this path. For instance, you can go to the sea shore. You can see a vast sea and gleaming bluish water all over, as far as your eyes can see. May be this will get you knowledge about the sea, but this is not the complete fact regarding the sea. The sea contains not just the water, there exists a different world under the sea water. So if you truly want pure knowledge of the sea, you need to go under the sea and see beyond the surface water which you see at first sight.

As I got off from the bus I looked around at all the sights and smells. I could see lots of people moving about, ahead I could see lots of ships and the boats. There were many shops too. Finally I realised that we were going to travel by a ship. I wanted to know what ship were we really going to travel by. Would it be small or big? Many such thoughts swirled in my head. As we queued up with our facilitators, I raised my head. There was a giant ship waiting for us. When I saw that enormous ship, I asked my facilitator, 'Is that the ship by which we are going to travel?' He answered dryly, 'Yes.' When I heard it, I quickly imagined the scene on board the *Titanic*, a film I saw once when I was in the orphanage. I looked at the ship and I could see similar people, fair and tall, who were walking on the deck, just like I had seen in the movie.

When I reached the gangplank, I looked around the ship. It was simply magnificent. It was very difficult to believe, especially for me. I had never ever seen such a giant object. It felt unreal. Inside, the ship was like a five star hotel. A floating city existed inside, where each and everything was there, for instance, different rooms for different travelers, a casino and a disco, and a swimming pool, a play hall for children, some shops and the immense dining hall were amazing. I roamed around for sometime, looking at everything. When I saw an elevator, I got into it. Some people were going downstairs in it. When we reached the lower deck, I could see lots of vehicles and a huge consignment of trucks. I was surprised and a mischievous idea came to me. I got into the elevator quickly and returned to the upper deck. I hurried to my room and asked my roommate Vishnu, 'Hey! Would you like to play football with me?' He thought I was crazy. Play football on a ship? Then he told me, 'Are you insane or what? Where the hell you going to play football on this ships?' I scoffed and chuckled at him and replied, 'You are such a jerk, you have not seen this giant and mind-blowing ship nicely. So come along with me, I'll show you the perfect ground where we can play football.' He was glaring at me with an open mouth and said, 'Fine, then let's go.'

I exclaimed in excitement, 'Here we go.' Both of us went downstairs in the elevator to play football. When we reached the bay where the trucks were parked, Vishnu was startled and said, 'Holy shit! How big a ship is it ? So many vehicles and consignment trucks lying over here.' I was smiling and behaving as if I never ever got astonished. I told him, 'This is nothing buddy. There are many thing you haven't seen in your whole life, alright?'

Then we began to play football, making continuous noise. The ball kept banging on the front mirrors and glass of the different vehicles. Soon we were perspiring and tired. Suddenly I heard a growling from behind. I halted and turned around. I could see a tall and chubby man, who was looking fiercely at both of us. So I asked that man, 'What happened, Sir?' and chuckled loudly. The fat man was very angry and said, 'You kids. Wait over there. Who the hell is going to pay if my car's glass breaks?' Then he began to move towards us menacingly. So quickly, I held the ball in my hand, and ran to the elevator. Vishnu too scampered behind me. We then ran to our room. When we reached the room, our hearts throbbed very fast and at the same time, we were laughing. I was afraid and wanted to be with an adult. I ran now to the facilitator from Nepal, Kabita. I just ran to her room and barged her door open, without knocking. In one chorus, voices yelled, 'Oh! No...No. Stop.' I was startled and then saw that her roommate, an American woman called Kimberly, had a towel wrapped around her. She was a friend of mine too.

I asked them in a surprised manner, 'What happened!' After a pause, the women began to laugh at me and Kimberly said, 'You should learn to knock on the door before getting into anybody else's room.' Everyone loved me very much, even Kimberly, but all of them were pretty much aware of my mischievousness and I guess, this also helped me win everyone's heart. When Kimberly asked me, 'What happened?' I replied in a casual way, 'Nothing. I just missed you guys, that's why I am here. Anyway, I'm going out. Okay then, bye... and Miss Kimberly, your towel has slipped down again.' Everyone's eyes turned to Kimberly, as I chuckled mischievously and ran way towards my own room. When I got into the room, Vishnu had gone to sleep. I woke him up and said, 'Come on man, get up. Don't sleep. We have to go for a swim now.' He replied in a low voice, 'What, man? It's a little cold. Anyway, where the hell will you go for swimming?'

I replied, 'Come on you deep shit, you haven't seen anything on this ship yet. Come with me to the swimming pool, it is on the deck, you got that?' He had no wish to swim and reluctantly said, 'Okay, lets go.' So we took some towels and ran to the deck. When we reached there, people were having coffee on the deck and it was really cold. But I wanted to swim even though I didn't know how to swim properly. But I knew very well that, I wouldn't get drowned. I mean I knew enough so as not to get drowned, so we stood by the pool and began to look at who was watching us. After a few minutes, I took off my clothes and dove into the swimming pool and immediately got out of it. The water was very cold and our ship was in mid-sea from where, we couldn't see anything other than the bluish water. I could see the vapour emitting from the mouth of people, talking to each other. My head and body were frozen and people leaning against the pool railings began to clap for both of us, for our bravado, trying to swim the cold and freezing water. I felt very cold and wanted to get out of the pool and run to our room, but by this time, people were looking at us and clapping for me, and the applause kept me in the pool. So I kept getting out and diving back into the cold water again and again. Vishnu couldn't tolerate the cold, so he put on his clothes, but I still kept swimming. Slowly people left the pool side. Only when everyone had left, I got out of the pool and ran towards the room. I was shivering so badly, my teeth chattered involuntarily. In the room, I wiped myself nicely with the towel and then put on warm clothes. After that I wrapped a blanket around myself. I was still shivering and sneezing very badly.

. After a while there was a call for dinner. When we gathered at the cafeteria, there was good news. The food was free for all the core marchers because the Captain of the ship had recognised the group from the electronic media and the newspaper coverages of the Global March. He was very happy to meet us and he said, 'You all children who are traveling by our ship are great, and I am very pleased today because you are traveling on my ship. I am extremely proud of you and all that you are doing, such noble work to safeguard the future of the world.' The Captain then went around, shaking each and everyone's hand. When we sat down at the dining table, the steward came and asked us to order. There were five of us at a table. I ordered fish and by chance it was the special dish of that day. We were flabbergasted by the big fish that came to the table. That day, we five core marchers, ate ten-kg of cooked fish, with glasses of fruit juices and sauces.

After finishing this delicious meal, I began to belch and everyone complained about my belches, 'Come on, what happened to you? Stop that,' and they laughed at me. I answered in my typical, brash manner, 'Come on everyone. You can't stop some things like pissing, loo, farting and belching. Am I right or wrong?' Everyone laughed uncontrollably and the whole cafeteria echoed with our laughter. Then I said, 'Okay then, ladies and gentlemen, I'm bushed and drowsy, so I am going to bed. Good night everyone.' I walked towards my room but when I tried to open the door, it would not open. The key was a card that I kept inserting, but couldn't succeed in opening the door. Finally, I went to the reception and sought help. The receptionist finally succeeded in opening my room's door.

When I lay down on the bed, Oh! My God, what a feeling! It was a very soothing and calm feeling. I could feel the floating of the ship. I could feel a sort of cradle and hear the very muted sound of the moving ship, like Mom is standing by my side, to sing lullabies. It was a great feeling and gradually, I went to sleep till we reached Greece.

ॐ॰ॐ॰

On The Aisle Of ILO

A small candle can rid of deadly darkness and a small log can save the life of a drowning person. The beautiful lotus grows in dirty water and diamonds can be found in coal mines. A puny ant can kill the elephant and tiny helpless children can bring about a revolution and show light to society, as being human beings, we all have the same rights to express ourselves. But the problem is that there are certain places where ordinary people can't imagine to be or even be for that matter. It was the first time in human history that we children — that too children who belonged to various low strata of this biased society — street children, orphans, victim of sexual harassment and bonded labourers, workers in dangerous cracker factories who lost their limbs due to negligence of the owners and domestic workers, all these children had gathered together to prove to the world that we are not ordinary and helpless. We were the part of the first ever Global March Against Child Labour. Though we were considered as 'unwanted' children who were neglected by society, we were out to prove that we had the potential to do miracles and change society and shake this world up. We were determined to eradicate child labour, and I had the good fortune to be an enthusiastic and willing campaigner.

From Greece to Switzerland, it was a fun trip for every core marcher. I would say, Switzerland was the best because it was the rendezvous for all other groups of core marchers to meet. The March had started from different corners of the world, like Asia, Africa and South/Latin America. When all the fighters for child rights gathered at Geneva, we shook Switzerland with our dynamic slogans.

The pain-filled voices of the children made the people of Europe aware of the value of children, who are the real future of the world. Resolutions to make a new law and rules for children of the whole world, were being made.

On Tuesday, 2nd June 1998, when hundreds of tiny steps approached the ILO building, shouting slogans, full of enthusiasm, the world couldn't figure out what

was really going on. It was a startling moment for
everyone. We were children who were not really able to
stand steadily on our feet. Our innocent eyes searched
for support to walk ahead. Our words were hesitant, our
voices were fearful but we remembered what Kailashji
had taught us six months ago — that in this world
where people, systems and governments conveniently
turn blind eyes and deaf ears to the silent sufferings of
child labourers, the courageous few have to step out
and fight for the rights of the vulnerable. That's why we
were marching towards ILO with our leader Kailashji,
demanding our right to food, education, justice and
equity. Our fight was for those millions of children in
different corners of the world who had to work and who
had no access to education and who suffered but could
not get any help. The astonishing thing was, we were in
the limelight and the focus of international media. We
didn't really mind them, we continued to chant, 'We
want...education! Go Go Global March... Stop... Stop...
Child labour! No more tools in tiny hands... We want
books and we want toys!' I still remember a boy, Khokon
from Bangladesh, who was one of the core marchers. He
did not have one leg, but he never quit walking with us
because he had fire in his heart and he felt very strongly
against child labour and the devastating effects that it has
on the lives of tender children. He was a living proof of

the curse that child labour could possibly perpetrate —
his leg is half amputated. Sometimes, he would stumble,
especially when jostled by the crowd but his indomitable
spirit always kept him on the go. I can recall each day
of the march — the man who conceptualised, executed
and led this behemoth of a March could hardly be seen
on the front row, unless called by the media or the local
organisers. He always ensured that Khokon led the
march and other children braced up immediately behind
him. Adults including all the leaders and facilitators were
always at the back end.

Today was the day. The world needed to hear the
stories of anguish and abandonment of all children that
we represented. And governments of 130 countries
needed to legislate against child labour and protect
children. I was just nine-years-old and I couldn't
remember everything but I know that I asked my
facilitator, Tarak Dhital, a question. 'Sir, is this the last
sensitisation campaign for people? Are they completely
aware how devastating child labour can get?' He said,
'Well...son, this is the main platform where various
governments of the different countries are going to
make laws to eliminate child labour.' I asked Tarakji,
'Why have they never ever thought about the rights of
children so far? Why do we little children have to fight
for our own rights? What is the duty of adults and the

governments towards us?'

Tarakji looked at me and grinned. 'Well...we are asking them the same question for a long time, but we haven't yet got any answers. You children are here for your own rights and this time they can't ignore you.' As we finished this conversation, Lily, a girl core marcher from Bangladesh passed by, shouting, 'Go... Go... Global March!! Stop... Stop... Child labour!! No more tools in tiny hands... We want books and we want toys!!' After that I shouted the same slogans and then passed the placard on to the other child core marcher, Govind Khanal, who was from Nepal but a representative from India. As he started raising slogans we were moving to the aisle of the ILO and towards the stage along with our leader Kailashji.

Representative of governments of various countries sat on chairs and looked towards us and some of them got up and stared at us in surprise. I don't really know what they were thinking about us but one thing was clear, that they were taken by surprise by this movement by children who were once child labourers.

We were a force that security guards and governments could not stop. We were in no mood to listen. We were chanting and raising slogans. We wanted to speak and speak — of those torments and social biases, of the pain of millions of child labourers and the unprivileged children because we were their only hope. That day, we were not begging for our rights and like Kailashji had always held, we were in complete control of the situation, demanding our own rights which society had snatched from us and which led to our exploitation. We rushed to the stage and then, all the core marchers sang a song in one voice. It was the song written by Kabita Aryal, who was also one of our facilitators from Nepal and I was the one who, with her, gave it the melody and the rhythm:

"Mm...hmm... We are children from different countries...

We are the children from different cultures...

But our problem is the same... that is child labour...

Our voice is the same... that is child labour.

Stop child labour...

Stop child labour...

Stop, stop, child labour...

We sing together... and dance together

We want education and we want to stop child labour.

But our problem is the same...

That is child labour.

Our voice is same...that is child labour.

Stop child labour...
Stop child labour...
Stops... stop... child... labour...

ೞೞೞ

Moment Of Truth

We finally entered the United Nations European Headquarters Palais des Nations in Geneva.

Then came the moment that all of us had been waiting for with baited breath. Kailash Satyarthi, along with all the core marchers, was invited to the stage. Now Kailashji was at the podium with representatives from governments, employers' organisations and workers' organisations from across the world at the 86th session of the International Labour Conference, eagerly waiting to hear from him.

Kailashji, in the capacity of Chair of Global March, delivered the most powerful speech ever. I wish I could reproduce his electrifying speech in its entirety, but I am putting down whatever I can remember or check with my friends and colleagues present at that time. Satyarthiji began his speech by saying,

'Today the real heroes are present here, who have reached here covering a distance that is double the periphery of the earth. Global March is the real transformation of moral power of most innocent victims into a worldwide movement that cannot be stopped now. If you cannot hear the loud slogans echoing between the earth and sky, history will never forget and forgive you. Today is the day to pledge and now is the moment to act.

'These children are not here for themselves, but to save the present and future of entire mankind. Every single footstep is not only a new script in the history, but a loud cry, an impatient rant and clarion call for urgent action. On behalf of 250 million child labourers we are here to tell you that childhood cannot wait any more. If you really believe that the world is not so poor, take away the tools, hammers, tongs and guns from their hands and give them books and pencils instead. If not, I opt to go back from here right away and can say goodbye with all humility for allowing us in for the first time in the history of United Nations and ILO, but I know and you know it as well — that a tiny portion of your annual military expenditure of 850 billion USD can bring freedom, smile and opportunities for the children of this world. You have to choose now between soldiers to fight and kill and teachers to save and build. What do you want to produce — bombs and guns or books and toys?

We are here to make a simple appeal. An international law to combat all exploitative forms of child labour through a new ILO Convention.

'The Global March has been able to generate an unprecedented level of public awareness. It has mobilised millions of people from all walks of life, including in those countries where the problem had never been recognised as an issue before. I am sure that this fire will not extinguish. Global March will spark off several children's movements against child labour as a result of the incredible participation of young people in the March. It has also given a new dimension to the culture of coalitions where NGOs, trade unions, religious groups, children's committees, governments, inter-governmental agencies, business communities and other concerned groups have joined hands in over 130 countries. Geneva has never been the final destination of the Global March. We will continue to march until the menace of child labour is completely wiped out from the face of humanity and every single child receives a free and meaningful education.'

Everybody was listening in pin drop silence. As Kailashji finished his speech, the entire hall burst into loud applause giving a standing ovation to him. My eyes did not blink once. I was on tenterhooks as Kailashji spoke. It was mesmerizing. Global March has undoubtedly been one of the the biggest congregations of our times.

Children like me and people from 130 countries had made it to the ILO after travelling over 80,000 kilometers across 103 countries of the globe, touching over 50 million people and mobilizing them against the crime and a social evil called child labour. As many as 7.2 million people donated their footprints as a mark of solidarity for the millions of children who languished in slavery. These footprints had been stacked as seven truckloads of paper. Our Global March received an overwhelming support from people from all walks of life. Some of the distinguished personalities who were a part of this historic march are the President of United States of America Bill Clinton, Prime Minister of United Kingdom Tony Blair, French President Jacques René Chirac, Indian President KR Narayanan, Queen of Spain, King of Belgium, Pope John Paul from Vatican City.

We spent two weeks more in Europe, after our March ended. I had made many friends during the march and we felt sad that the event was finally coming to an end. It was time for each one of us to return to our respective countries.

சுஜஜஞ

From Kathmandu To India

*N*owadays, we can see that most people are aware of child rights and child labour. Today, whenever I sit down on the porch, I feel good that I was a part of that children's movement and finally we brought some sort of a revolution in this world, so that other destitute children can live better lives. This is the real achievement of my life and I'm proud of it, because being a child labourer, I could give back something to this world.

When darkness covers society and humanity starts to quench the thirst of selfishness, then the world needs one small way out, one little aperture from where ordinary people can save their rights and understand values of clichés like 'Live and let live.' To establish justice in society there is need for one strong candle to remove the darkness and show the path to the unprivileged, the exploited and the downtrodden. This way, they receive a light of *hope and a glimpse of the freedom that they can have.*

This flickering candle was Kailash Satyarthi and that candle was burning and glowing the light of freedom, known as Mukti Ashram.

I decided to hold on to the hand of the person who always admired me and spoke about me at the Global March movement. I had grown very fond of him. In fact, I tagged along with him from the very beginning to end of the march. I don't know what he saw in me. I still wonder about that, but he was fond of me and he always treated me as a special person. Kailash Satyarthi is the chairperson of the Global March Against Child Labour and the founder of Bachpan Bachao Andolan. He lived in Delhi (India). I lived in Kathmandu. So, in 1999, I made up my mind to move to New Delhi, the capital of India, to be close to him. At the back of my mind was also the knowledge that my father was Indian. I had a family somewhere in India. I had to get to India.

I was just ten years old, a little boy who decided to travel from Nepal to India alone, in search of Kailashji.

After six months of traveling the world, I had returned to CWIN, with the CWIN team, facilitators and children from Nepal. By now I was very famous; all the Nepali media — television, radio and newspapers — covered me; each and every day there would be an interview with me; I had to speak everywhere. It was as if I was a celebrity. Then I got an advertisement spot. It was a television advertisement that used to come on daily on TV and it was about eradicating child labour. The ad showed a child working in a hotel, a child as a domestic servant and a child picking rags. It seemed as if I had a 'famous' life. Suddenly some teachers and activists felt that I was getting all the glory and fame and not CWIN, the organisation. They began to advocate that I should be expelled from the rehab Home that sheltered me. Now, after having this beautiful life, how could I imagine going back to the street?

It was as if a beautiful dream was coming to an end. I felt threatened, betrayed, insecure. To hide my real feelings, I began to tell everyone that I wanted to go India. I made drawings which showed the flag of India. Every picture I drew had a path that travelled from Nepal to India. The flag of India was everywhere. This disappointed the Nepali NGO more. I did not know anything about nationalism at that time. I just knew that India was my country, because somewhere I knew that it is the country of my dad, because he was Indian, so I wanted to go to India. And when I thought of India, I saw Kailashji's face. So, one fine morning I made up my mind to leave Nepal, to go to my dad's country.

I already had a fair idea of the land route to take. I had once taken the bus ride to Veerat Nagar. I had also travelled the overland route from Bangladesh to Nepal to India with the CWIN team, as a part of the Global March group.

During the Global March, all of us participant children used to get a weekly pocket money of seven dollars. I had saved this money. When I returned to Kathmandu, I had bought the most expensive bicycle, I could. It was my dream bicycle. But when I decided to go India, the first thought that came to my mind was to sell this cycle and get travel money. During the Global March, I had accumulated a lot of gifts too. I had a pair of skates, which I got from Italy. And lots and lots of clothes and souvenirs from all around the world. For a whole week I just keep thinking how should I take all this to India? I found that all my stuff put together would be really heavy. How would I carry all of this? So, I just took the diary, where I used to write my everyday thoughts and happenings, and the addresses of important people. In this notebook was one page where Kailashji's address and picture was there.

First I sold the bicycle. And early one morning, I decided to run away from CWIN's Transitory Rehabilitation Centre A.

I boarded a bus from Kathmandu to Bhairawa, and then to Sunauli. From here, I managed a ride on a jeep that took me to Gorakhpur, in India. Many travelled this way. When I reached Gorakhpur, I asked people where the bus to Delhi was. People showed me the bus. But when I went to the bus conductor and tried to take out money from my pocket for the ticket to Delhi, I did not find a single penny in my pocket. This time, I was quite scared.

Earlier, on the streets of Kathmandu, my bravado had come from my ignorance. Now I had become aware. I had been a Global Marcher Against Child Labour. Now I realised what a very small and insignificant person I was. And I had heard lots of stories of missing children and how they get trafficked and kidnapped. I knew martial arts, so I thought I'd manage to fight with people trying to kidnap me. But, on the other hand, I was small and knew that if five big-built people came to take me, then how would I fight with them? Such questions kept roaming in my head. Whenever people at the bus stand came near me, I would avoid them. Sometimes people tried to talk to me, ask me, 'Where do you want to go?' I would not speak. I would run away from them. At times, I would get angry and answer them, 'It's none of your business.' Somewhere I had developed a defensive instinct.

I realised that my money had finished. So, from the bus stand I found out and moved to the Gorakhpur Railway Station. I walked to a *dhaba* here and hoped I could ask for food and some money. I hoped there would be some good soul around who would help me. However, several people deflected me, saying, 'Don't make me a fool, okay? You people keep coming around to fool us.' Some others said, 'Money does not come free. You have to earn it.' I understood soon that people would not help me. Then I decided to find some work. But when I asked for work, people looked at me, in a kind of surprised manner. I did not look like a destitute. I looked like a child from a well-to-do household.

Appearances mattered. I had begged, I had worked. But, now, a little educated, I had been a globetrotter who had participated in Global March Against Child Labour in several countries.

I looked like a child from a middle-class family. So, I created a story on the spot. I spoke to people about my problem. I told them that my money had finished and I needed to go to my uncle and aunt's place. I showed them Kailashji's picture. One person somehow believed me. This man desperately needed a small child to do his dish washing. He ran a *dhaba* and he agreed to let me work for one month and pay me at the end of the month. He said, he would feed me and let me sleep in his *dhaba* and he showed me the place where I'd do the dishes. He gave me to eat and told me the work would start at 4 pm. I had a sense of playing out a tape once again.

After I had eaten, I washed my plate and I went near to the counter to keep back the plate. I could see behind the counter and realised that the drawer was open and the money inside was visible. I was not a thief. But I also knew people would not help, if I asked for money honestly. I didn't want to follow the path which I had already left. So I made up my mind to take only as much as I needed, when no one was looking. I soon had my chance. At the opportune moment, I grabbed just a thousand rupees, and picking up my luggage, I ran towards the bus station, because I didn't know how to travel in the train to Delhi. This time, my heart beat faster than when I used to be just a street child. Many thoughts swirled in my mind, mostly of fear. I had stolen money, and I feared I would be chased. One man shouted, 'Hello!' and I thought, 'Oh! Shit. I'm dead.' I didn't stop running. Then, suddenly, I bumped into a man and fell down. This man said, 'Hey Hey Hey! Where are you going in such hurry?' I didn't know what to say, I thought somebody had caught me. But, as I looked back, there wasn't anybody running after me. So I replied, 'Somebody said the bus to Delhi is just going from that side, and I'm in hurry.' The man smiled and said, 'No, no. Look at that bus. It is going towards Delhi. You don't have to run.' I smiled and said, 'Oh! Thank you, Sir.' Then as I sat in the bus, from inside, I just kept looking outside, to see if anybody was coming to catch me.

When the bus started to move, I began to hide myself. Suddenly the conductor came and said, 'You don't have money or what?' I pretended to smile and said, 'What do you think? Am I going to travel to Delhi, hiding from you? Ha, ha. I have a stomach ache actually.' I offered him the money and said, 'Here is the money for the ticket to Delhi. How much is it?' He replied, 'Don't worry. I will not take more from you than from the others.' I smiled and said, 'I know you can't take more because my dad has prepared me a lot before I came here. He has told me each and everything about bus fares and from where I would get the bus to Delhi.' He then asked me, 'Are you alone?' I said, 'Yes. I'm a grown up child. I can travel alone.' A woman near by giggled and said, 'Yes, we can see how big you are.' The woman asked me, 'Where are you going to in Delhi?' I showed her the picture of Kailashji and said, 'I'm going to my uncle and aunt's house, because I miss them very much. So, my dad sent me and he has told them from where they would have to pick me up.'

When the conductor gave me the ticket, I decided not to talk with anybody and I just pretended to go to sleep. I didn't eat anything when the bus stopped for a break. I just got out to pee, then got back into the bus and just went to sleep. When I reached the Vasant Vihar bus terminal in Delhi, I got off the bus but I didn't know how to go to Kailasji, and where to go.

৩৫৫৫

Mukti Ashram

However, at the back of one of the photographs of the Global March, there was a phone number. The number was of the Mukti Ashram. I had taken that number and address from one boy who was a participant in the Global March. He had come from Bachpan Bachao Andolan's rehabilitation centre, the Mukti Ashram, in north Delhi.

So I asked one STD booth person to dial this number. One staff member of the Ashram responded to the call. He gave me directions on how to get to the Mukti Ashram. From the Gorakhpur-Delhi terminus I was told to take a bus for ISBT Delhi. From ISBT I took the bus to Nathupura, where Mukti Ashram is. From there it was not difficult to find Kailashji. I reached Mukti Ashram and then was escorted to Kailashji house.

Seeing me at their doorstep Kailashji and his family were really very surprised. Kailashji asked me to stay at his home and called me his son. I stayed with him for a few days and had a really good time with the family. But I wasn't a boy who had ever really lived at home. My life had been astray. So I told them, I did not want to stay at home. He then decided to send me to live at Mukti Ashram. Mukti Ashram is a short-term rehabilitation centre of Bachpan Bachao Andolan for the rescued child bonded-labourers, where they stay and are counseled to tide over the hardship and exploitation these children faced in life. Elementary reading, writing and number skills are also imparted to the rescued child labourers before they are repatriated by the law enforcement agencies back to their parents.

Mukti Ashram was a really beautiful place. As a new child, I was enthusiastically welcomed by lots of other children. My head spun. I saw flowers at the edges of the playgrounds and trees all over. It was like a hill station. The dormitories were built like traditional huts, of mud and bricks but they were beautiful. Children living at the Mukti Ashram were learning the values of nature and to respect each and every resource from nature. Nature itself teaches us freedom and this is the real lesson one has to learn from nature. As I started to live in this rehabilitation centre, I learnt that this was the place where I and children like me could become free from a selfish and victimising world. Teachers here were dedicated to the children. I was also very happy here, I was liked by other children. They gave me hope and taught me the importance of my existence.

Every day other children would come to me to learn something new, because they liked me the way I was. The most important part of that was, I was one of them, a former child labourer as they saw me. And they wanted to be like me. That was the reason Satyarathiji sent me to this rehabilitation centre, to understand myself and understand the value of my existence. He made me understand that living just for one's own self is worthless. But fighting for others' lives makes a person worthy. He taught me the way he used to be, and somehow, he spotted the talent in me and became my real mentor, my Hero. He decided to involve me in each and every activity which his organisation Bachpan Bachao Andolan (that he founded in 1980) held through this institution, like Children's Parliament and several others. That year, the parliament was held in New Delhi and children came from different parts of India and we discussed the importance of education and the poor state of government schools. We learnt that there were many schools in villages which were roofless and children were not going school but teachers were merely filling their attendance sheets. After these discussions, we made a presentation to a High-level Committee where celebrities were present. I was the one who did the presentation in that high-level meeting and the education minister sat beside me. So, after participating in countless such events and campaigns, I began to give leadership to the movement. I learnt much in the process.

I was guided and given many opportunities by Kailashji, who treated me like his son. I spent a few eventful years in Mukti Ashram and understood the true worth of this place. It wasn't an ordinary place like other centres and shelter Homes. This centre was different. It gave children the self-confidence that they had lost during many traumatic events in their lives. This place gave voiceless and frightened children their voice back. It brought smiles on their faces when they came in tears and terrified and battered. I still remember one incident at the Mukti Ashram. One day, I was taking class. The children in the class were newcomers, they had been rescued from bonded labour. I asked a boy to turn off the lights. He threw a slipper at the bulb to put it off. I was simply amazed that in the 21st century also, there are people unaware of electricity. At times we found shoes and slippers inside the refrigerator. I've seen children who really came from the back of beyond and were brought to the mainstream with the help of education. I was fascinated by the way Kailashji interacted and engaged with these children.

That transitory rehabilitation centre was also home to a heterogeneous lot. You could see here children coming from different cultures, religions and different part of the country. Some were rescued from brick kilns, carpet industries, domestic services and some were from stone quarries. When they entered the Ashram, I could see very frightened faces. It was like, somewhere, they had lost the hope to live and dream. But after a few days at Mukti Ashram, they would slowly begin to participate in each and every activity happening at the Ashram. They sang and danced, studied and they joked and played. They had got back brand new lives and felt alive, perhaps for the first time in their lives. I was very happy to be with these children. They were not dumb, they could do everything, all that a normal regular human being could do. They just needed one opportunity and there was this possibility of miracles happening.

They too had dreams. I heard their stories full of pain. But at the end, they would share their dreams. Someone would say, 'I wish I were a doctor, a teacher, lawyer.' I saw their every possible dream. I understood them very well because somewhere, I was emotionally connected to them and whatever they were sharing with me, for me it became my own story that I had shared with someone or the other. I still remember the day we were sitting and talking to each other. An eight-year-old boy called Ashraf Ali told me how he had been working as a domestic help in a senior police officer's home. One day he was starving because nobody gave him food. So he drank some left over milk. He was brutally beaten for that. Sometime after that, he was rescued by BBA and brought to Mukti Ashram. My story resonated with his.

This is what I liked the most about Kailashji and his Indian organisation, Bachpan Bachao Andolan. They brought smiles back into the lives of distressed little children. As Kailashji treated me like a son, later on some people in Mukti Ashram became very jealous. He often told me, 'Hey! Son, mark my word, that day is not far when you'll be a famous and renowned person. Keep working hard because somewhere my heart keeps telling me that you have that potential to do something.' He knew all that I could do: dancing, acting, writing and martial arts. I had a dream — to become an actor and I was working very hard to enhance my skills in these arts. I was confident that one day I'll rock this world.

That's how I interacted with a lot of people. They used to be really appreciative and surprised by my opinions, because we had age gap of twice or even more. This also made me feel that I'm also an important person in this world. I soon began to hang around with the foreigners, people like Alam Rahman. He was, by then, a very good friend. We had visited many countries together during the Global March. I used to call him Brother. He taught me many things and I used to go with him to the sports complex and we used to have lots of fun. Whatever he taught me was fun too.

৪০ৎ৪০ৎ

Boomerang Of Life

Like I met Alam, Global March gave me yet another friend for a lifetime. I met Dori Santolaya. Dori was one of the volunteers at Global March International Secretariat in Delhi. At any point in time there used to be over a dozen international volunteers besides several local volunteers. Dori became a good friend too. One day she said, 'Basu, I've seen many children but they are not as lucky as you are. You've got lots of experience in your life. You should start writing a diary and who knows, one day, you'll be able to tell the world what it is like to be a street child and what the situation is actually for destitute children.' From that day onwards I started to keep a diary. Dori even helped with my studies. In 2005, I decided to leave the Mukti Ashram because I had some differences of opinion with the director of the centre. By that time, I was in high school and I was much more confident than in the past. I, along with a few more adolescent boys, were shifted to another accommodation in the vicinity of Mukti Ashram in Burari, by the organisation.

Later on we decided to choose our own path.

As Kailashji got to know of my decision to leave the new accomodation, he was very saddened. He made me promise that I would always keep in touch with him. Whenever he called me home, I had to be there.

When I was a child, my life was on the street. But here, now, I was educated and sophisticated. And I did not know how life would be for a high school teenager. What sort of life there would be? Or would he be able to survive in the professional world? Here I had to start my life all over again, like a small new-born baby. But this much I knew. I was going to live. Once my life was on the street and I had to do different jobs to survive. I knew how. Today I had a sense of self-worth, how important I had been, I knew of man's value but the world I was going to face was totally new and my dream was brand new too.

So, with the hope of fulfilling my dreams, I started a new journey of life, all the while wondering what would happen to my dream? Would I get success? Whenever you take a step ahead to do something which you've just imagined like a dream, it is really hard to prove it in reality, but not impossible.

The journey of life had never been very easy for me.

But now, in 2005, I started another one. I had built some connections around the world during my stay at Mukti Ashram and my regular visits to Global March Secretariat. I had some good friends like Dori Santolaya from Spain, Alex Sagarra from Switzerland and Alam Rahman from Canada. I used to share my feelings with these friends and they used to always support me. It is the era of the cyber world and internet so I made myself computer savvy. After all, this was the only way that I could connect with people who wanted me to keep in touch with them, so they could e-mail me and I would be able to reply.

I already believed that whosoever showed me a little love, care and concern were all my family. I didn't have any expectation from the people I knew. I did not think they would help me like family, and I was pretty much aware that I was just an orphan. I imagined a family. It was raining heavily but I was the only one on whom not a single drop of water fell. There was a crowd outside but I was just walking alone. I would walk through people. They just looked at me like you see the things around you while you are walking, but you are not really interested nor want to remember what you see. I was the only one who existed for myself alone. I understood that I needed to change myself in a wise way, because I needed the knowledge and understanding rather than the changes in life I had seen.

When I left Mukti Ashram, in the beginning I had to

spend some nights on the street again. It was as if I had been the most important person for nothing. I remembered those days when I was in the movement known as the Global March Against Child Labour. It was the time when people made me realise that I was a very important person, sitting among very important people of the world who took big decisions in their countries. I got a lot of applause and a lot of respect and five star hotels to stay in. There would be hot water, bedrooms and cars according to the country I was in and all the electronic and print media would run after me to interview me. How I used to run away from them. It was very strange that life kept playing games with me. The best of times and the worst of times. A see-saw. This time, when I slept on the roadside, there wasn't any media. Not even a stray dog to take note. The bus shelter was the most comfortable room I could get. It was as if my past life did not want to leave me. I now remembered all those friends on the streets of Kathmandu with whom I spent my long, long childhood days.

One thing kept bothering me, would my life end like this?

I had my answer though, this time. I am meant to do something and people who liked me during my journeys through different countries and being part of an exemplary movement were trying to teach me something. There had always been a strange thing in my life. I had to give an exam first and learn the lesson afterward. People go to school, college and universities and learn and then give exams. As there were no parents and schools to guide me, time took a hand. Time had different ways of teaching. So exam first; if you survive, then you get the knowledge.

ဆဝသ၆သ၆

Marking Up

After the Global March, I had spent a lot of time requesting people to provide education to those children who had taken part in the March to reform society. However, I had never included myself among them. I never had any sort of expectation for myself. I was just happy that at least I had got the chance to travel the world and had got lots of love from those beautiful people who I had met on the March. It made me realise that all human beings are not selfish. There are people around the world who do care about those who are needy and who are in trouble. I understood that those are the people because of whom, humanity still exists.

After living in the park and bus station for a few days, I got a mail from Dori and she said that she had sent me some money for my accommodation. I was very happy and blessed her from the core of my heart. I hardly pray and I never prayed for myself. That time I just closed my eyes and called God, to whom I have been introduced by people of this world. I called out to this God and prayed for Dori. When I got the money, I searched for accommodation and continued going to school. By now I was wondering what I was really going to do? 'How am I gonna survive?'

Someone told me about the Business Process Outsourcing (BPO) companies. So I tried my luck there. I went for the interviews. I didn't get selected because I was an undergraduate. And I failed ten interviews. I broke down again.

I decided to tell lies and went to a cyber cafe and changed my resume. I just paid ten rupees to the cyber cafe guy to become a graduate in my resume. Now I was no more just a high school boy. I wanted to keep my honesty but I needed a job more. I had to protect myself from returning to the street. I didn't want to get involved in any bad business, the way I had in my so-called childhood. I was just completing my high school education and it was hard to get a job in India without graduation. I could not go for a very low salary and I wanted to present myself as an educated and sophisticated guy. So, this time, I went for the BPO interview for the eleventh time, wearing a formal dress and with a smile on my lips.

HR asked me to sit and fired a question at me

immediately: So tell me something about yourself.

I smiled and greeted the human resource staff of the company interviewing me first. Then I said, 'As you know, my name is Basu Rai and I have done my high school from Joseph and Mary Public School. I have completed my graduation from Delhi University, and now I'm pursuing my master's from the same university. As far as my family is concerned, they have a toy factory business in Norwich, England. I have been born and brought up there only.

'If you ask me about my interest, I like Martial arts, Music and Dance. That's all about me Ma'am.'

After my pitch, the male HR asked me another question: 'Why you are in India?' I replied in a calm way, 'Well.. Sir... my Grandpa and Grandma are here in Delhi and I want to stay with them forever, because they love me a lot.' The lady HR gave me the Offer Letter for the job as a customer executive. I learnt that day that to survive in this world, you really need to be smart. It was not the first time that I was surviving, but my strategy of smartness was new. Sometimes, your honesty brings you on the road and keeps you unemployed. Instead of finding your capabilities, people look for degrees. My question was, if as a teenager, I could work as customer executive in a very good manner, then why did I have to lie to just get the job?

When I started to work in the call centre, there were more difficulties. I was working in the UK process and had to work in the mortgage department. I, thus, learnt that many people who were living in England were living on mortgage and bankers would make false promises to switch their mortgages, just to make money. You kept disturbing people even when they were ill or somebody had died in their family. As a call centre guy, I had to keep calling and harassing them. Once, I called one gentleman. He picked it up and said, 'Hello!' As I got a reply, I started to give him my pitch and said, 'Hi! Am I speaking with Mr David?' I got a prompt reply in a very low voice, as if some one at the other end was very sad. I was trained to ignore anything personal, so I again said, 'Hi! David, I'm Martin and speaking from the bank. We know that you have taken mortgage right?' The man replied, 'Yes.' I got the idea that the guy still had the mortgage. So I delivered the next line of my pitch: 'See, we have an offer for you since we can see your mortgage interests are very high. We value your hard earned money, which we need to take care of. So, if you switch your mortgage with our bank you'll have less interest to pay and even your redemption charge will be taken care of by us. It means you don't have to pay a single penny if you chose the option to switch your mortgage with us.' As I finished, the man started to cry . He said, 'Why you people don't understand, today my wife is dead and I just got back home from her funeral. I'm going through very hard emotional times. Do you guys fu… care about it or just you guys enjoy calling and stealing my money?' As I heard this sentence from the man, I couldn't control myself and some tear drops rolled down from my eyes. Then I offered him my deep condolence and said that I was very sorry. But this man just cried and cried. After a few minutes, he said, 'I am sorry. I'm not in a position to talk about mortgage right now.' I replied, 'No problem Sir. Please take good care of yourself.' Then I hung up the phone. I realised how nicely this gentleman was talking to me even when he was so terribly distressed.

This incident kept troubling me whenever I sat on calls. Soon I left the job. I began to understand that even as I was working hard to make a living, those English people who had greater family responsibilities, were being trapped and our bankers were taking advantage of their compulsion and stealing their money. We at the call centre were just giving them a buzz, contracted to do so. We had no understanding of their problems.

I switched jobs to an American company and used to sell medicines like viagra and cealis and many more such medications. The call centre's life was really, really strange for me. I had to keep awake the whole night and sleep in the day. I used to have lots of problems like ear pain, body aches and headaches. I could see girls and boys were drinking and smoking cigarettes to stay awake and work. I couldn't drink because I used to follow what the books said — that I shouldn't drink till I was more than eighteen years old. However, I read a lot about the benefits and harms of alcohols, beers and cigarettes but I didn't touch anything to stay awake. I soon came to know that these BPOs were in India because infrastructures was cheap and people were ready to work 24/7 because of unemployment, huge population and these companies were simply exploiting these employees because we were working for America but getting paid according to minimum wages of India. The companies showed eight hours of work time but made us work for twelve hours or sometimes more, to complete our targets. While working in the night, employees went through lot of health problems too.

After three years of call centre work, I decided to quit the job and do something else. I decided to teach English. I did a little research about the kind of English language problems people in Delhi faced. I discovered people had problem with American and British pronunciation and spellings. So I decided to open an institute by the name, the American and British Institute of Lingua Franca. Well... I knew that I didn't look like a teacher because I was just a short guy who didn't look like a teacher from any angle. But I had one important thing, that is confidence and my acting skills.

ဆဝ⚭ဝ⚭

The English Teacher

I had little money. So I started with some friends. They began to attend my classes. They got good results in three months. So I got more confident and began guaranteeing that I could teach English within three months. Soon I started to have a variety of students. Some were school students. Some were graduates, some were managers and employees of companies who were double my age and more educated. In the beginning, I was a little nervous. But as I recalled my street life, I thought that in comparison, this was a better choice. I used to charge them one thousand rupees for a month. Gradually, the number of the students increased and I began to earn a good amount of money.

I was really short in height, about 5' 3" and looked like a school student. My students used to ask me questions like, where are you from? I used to reply, 'I'm from England.' Oh! Shit, it was a hard thing to believe but I was a little fair guy and I took a chance. 'So, What your mom and dad do?' I would reply, 'My parents have really big toy factories from where they send electronic and many other toys all around the world.' They would ask me a lot of things about England and I used to surf the internet to know more about England. Sometimes I would say things like, 'you know what? I never liked England. I always liked India. I might have more knowledge of England, compared to India. It's natural.' Thank God, they never asked me what was the name of my dad's company, otherwise, in the confusion, I am sure I would have said, whatever softwares Bill Gate is using, my dad sells him, ha, ha! The way I used to dress up and talk in broken Hindi, they believed me. That was the part of my acting. Sometimes they would ask me to speak in Hindi, so I used to speak, '*aap kinaam ki he*' and they laughed and corrected me. 'Ha, ha... No, no, Sir. That's wrong. Say in this way, *aap ka naam kya hai*?' I would say, 'Oh! I was very close, no?' My students would laugh.

Since childhood, I always wanted to become an actor. I never imagined that I'd actually act to survive. The English teacher was the character I had to play in my real life. It wasn't true that my Hindi was bad. I could speak excellent Hindi but I used to pretend. That was funny and I used to be scared to do that too, because inside, I knew I was making a fool of people. Now, I was no more known as Basu Rai. I had changed my name and my name was Alex Roger. I have absolutely no idea how this name popped up in my mind. This gave people the impression that I was really an English guy, not an Indian. One day, one of my students asked me to show him my passport. I smiled at him and said, 'I wish I could get my passport.' The students quickly asked me, 'Why Sir?' Oh! Why? Sad story actually. 'My grandma treats me as a baby. Do I look like a baby to you guys?' Students: 'No Sir.' I smiled and replied, 'But, unfortunately, my grandma does and she is very much concerned about my losing it. So she has asked me, whenever I go to England, she would come with me to the embassy and would give my passport back, when I board the plane. See, last time I wanted to take my cell phone sim card, I had to ask one of my friends, Basu Rai, to give me his ID proof. So, if you call to the call centre of the sim card company, they will mention Basu Rai rather than Alex Roger. But he has asked me to promise him that I should not cause him any problem.' After that, my students started to laugh. So, people had doubts sometimes, but I used to clear their doubts in a very smart way.

I was famous with the girls too. They liked me, so I used to go to parties, people used to invite me for lunch and dinner. One day I got an invitation to have lunch with one of my students and his friends. When I reached the venue, I could see two beautiful women with my student. I had lunch with them and one girl who looked like a foreigner. Originally she belonged to a state known as Himachal Pradesh. She became friendly. The girl really had a good figure, her colour was fair, hair colour was a little brown and definitely, she was taller than me. She was quite impressed with my conversation. My student, who was older than me, asked us to exchange cell phone numbers. We all did that. She started to call me daily. I used to be very busy but I would take out some time to talk to her. After all, she was pretty.

But one time, it was a day off in my institution. I heard a knock at the door. I saw six tall and muscular guys standing outside. As a courtesy, I asked them, 'Yes, may I help you?' One tall guy in the team said, 'We are here to talk to Alex Roger.' I was happy that I had got some more students. So I called them in. They sprawled out in the room and one guy asked me, 'Do you know Mina?' I was a little shocked but not that much. I replied, 'Yes. I do know her.' They looked at each other and one guy asked me, 'How do you know her?' I replied, 'That's not your business. Now you tell me why are you here?' One guy came forward and said, 'Mina is my girlfriend.' I understood that these boys were here to beat me, not to get taught by me. I feared, I was going to be beaten in front of everyone. Since I was a nice teacher and people who had institutions around were very fond of me, I decided to lock the door from the inside and I threw the key somewhere in the corner and sat down on my chair again. Those boys were looking at me in a strange manner. After sitting, I asked them a question, 'Tell me one thing boys. did you see the signboard which is hanging outside of my institution's wall?' They looked at me and replied in a small voice. 'Yes. We have seen, but why are you asking?' I smiled at them and said, 'If you have noticed, I give special classes for self-defence too.'

'But before coming to any conclusion, let me ask you why you are here, and what has this girl said to you?' The boyfriend of the girl said, 'Actually, caught your sms one day. So she got scared and told me each and every thing immediately. She said, you harass her a lot. She doesn't know you but you keep calling her.' I didn't know that somebody would say such things about me. I asked him to call her in front of me. He called her, I asked him to put the call on speaker. He asked the girl, 'Does Alex harass you?' She replied, 'I don't know him. I have never met him, but he keeps calling me.' So I asked him to put off the phone and took out my sophisticated cell phone, an Android LG P500, that was the first Android smart cell phone I had, and in it showed her picture and mine, which were taken together and stored. In that picture, she was hugging me and sitting on my lap. That was proof that she had met me, knew me. This really shocked the lover boy.

Then I took a knife from my table. They looked at me in a very strange way. I told them, 'You know what I'm going to do? Stab this knife into myself and I am going to call the cops on you. You all are finished, my friends.' They got so worried, they said, 'Sir... you took it so seriously. We were here to only talk to you.' I replied in great anger, 'Are you talking to me? Do I look like that stupid to you guys? To speak to a single person, you don't need six tall and heavy muscular guys. I doubt that you know that one of my uncles is here in Delhi and he is a police officer and his rank is that of SHO (Station House Officer).' Honestly, I didn't know the full form of that abbreviation at that time. I said, 'If something happens to me, you guys are already dead. He will sue you for attempt to murder me.'

They started to say sorry and asked me to open the lock of the door. I took a lot of time. I was scaring them as much as possible, so they would not attack me in the future. Finally, I opened the door. As I opened the door, they just walked away without saying anything. It was as if they had just saved their lives. But if you ask me, I would say that I felt lighter and felt thankful that I was still in one piece. After that, I called Mina's elder brother and said, 'Hi! my name is Alex Roger. I hope you remember me. Once I called your sister and you picked up the phone and I pretended to be an institution teacher. Actually your sister and I have an emotional relationship and I didn't know that she already had a boyfriend. She was playing with both of us and today she sent him to beat me up, along with five other guys. So, if you have time, please come to meet me, otherwise I'm going to file a case on your sister for attempting to murder me.' Mina's big brother was in panic and said, 'Sir. I will definitely come to meet you. Please don't file any case on her without talking to me.' I said, 'Okay. I'll be waiting for you at my institution.' Then I gave him the address.

He came to me and I explained each and everything to him. I knew the Indian tradition, so I showed him her picture, taken together with me. His face was red with shame and he said, 'I'm very sorry Sir... and it won't happen in the future.' I took this step of involving the brother because I knew there would be the possibility that the girl would send back those boys again. So I played a smart game here. After that, I never had any problem with any girl.

My institution was booming, but it wasn't a perfect institution. There was just one room which I had partitioned into two parts, with beautiful curtains hanging around. On one side, I had my bed and on the other side I used to run my institution. Nobody could figure out that it was my residence too. People used to like my institution for another reason too. Every week, I used to throw a party. I would announce on Friday that on Sunday, we are going to have party that would be a beer-and-barbecue party. So whosoever wanted to be a part of it, please put your names on a list and contribute to the expense. So Sunday used to be fun day for my students. They would get drunk and listen to my favourite American country music. And they spoke in broken English, without any hesitation. So this was one smart way to bring the students into the institution, and do my business too.

Every student who came to my institution, had one common complaint: 'We learnt English from so and so institution.... I couldn't speak English. Yet, how can you teach us English within three months, Sir?' I would smile and tell them, 'I've taught English to an animal. You are a human. It will be very easy for me.' The students would think I was joking. So students would say, 'An animal? No, Sir. That is not possible.' I would smile again and would call my puppy. His name was Leopard. I would call out, 'Leopard! come here!' My Leopard would wake up and turn his head around and look at me, then come to me. I would ask Leopard to shake hands with my students, and this cute Leopard would look at the students and shake hands with them. As they began to comprehend, I would tell Leopard, 'Okay, Leopard, my boy. Thank you very much. Now c'mon, get back to your place.' Leopard would rise and go back to his place and sit. I would reiterate, 'So you see. An animal, and I have taught him English successfully. For me you'll be very easy.' They used to smile at me like I was crazy. They would, however, fill the forms and pay me. It was as if for the first time in their lives they had found a real teacher. Of course, a little crazy, keeps animal to give demo and compares people with him.

ೲಀೢೲೢಁ

Dark And Lonely

I never thought that Leopard would be my partner in teaching. I was a loner. To get away from loneliness, I would drink beer, sometimes hard liquor with some so-called friends. But at the end of the evening, they would go back home to their families and I would remain alone. Just alone in one room and the loneliness of that room used to eat me from within. So I thought I would buy a puppy. I went to a pet shop, I saw lots of puppies, and the shop showed me different breeds too. The puppies looked well-fed and well looked-after. One small, skinny pup started playing with my boots. I picked him up and started to play with him. The dog's owner asked me, 'Would you like to see other puppies too?' I said, 'No! But I'm taking this guy.' The pet shop owner gave me a surprised look and asked me for conformation, 'Are you sure sir?' Nobody had liked this puppy because he was skinny and looked ugly. I told him, 'No, he is cute, and I'm taking him.' The pet shop's owner looked at me and said, 'Well. It will cost you seven thousand only, other pets are a little more expensive, but if you want to take him, I could give you in a little lesser price.' I brought this guy home and started to share with him my thoughts, and play with him and I called him 'Leopard.' The name came to me because he was black and I had seen a black leopard in a movie. So I gave him this name and hoped that he would be as dangerous as a real leopard but he was really gentle, friendly and social as he grew up.

Leopard was just a month old, so I had to take care of him a lot. He used to piss and shit around in my room and I had to clean it up, because the room was also used for the English classes. I had to maintain hygiene as much as possible. Leopard used to sleep with me, and in winter, the bugger would piss on me. Suddenly I would have to get up and take a bath, change my bed sheet and I even had to give him a bath because he didn't like to sleep alone. Whenever I used to make him sleep in his bed, he would cry. So I didn't have any choice. Sometimes, I would get fed up with him but I had taken the responsibility of his life, so no choice. But gradually, Leopard was growing and I taught him many things, like finding hidden things, fetching a ball, taking his shit outside, shaking hands and, of course, he learnt English too.

It's not that I didn't have friends. I had lots of friends.

I had heard that rich people's children have more etiquette, so I wanted to improve my moral science and etiquette. I started to chose my friends from those who had Mercedes Benz and BMWs, that used to be my way of identifying rich guys. Somehow, they liked me and we would become good friends. I would hang around with these guys. Their daily lives were really strange, getting up late, going to college and coming home and taking a little nap. And in the night, drinking at the bar and dancing. This would be their schedule. They had lots of girlfriends too.

These guys would treat me very well because I earned lots of money. I would get help from my friend Dori Santolaya. She would send money for my education and accommodation. Whatever money I earned, I used all of that to go to pubs and drink. I never used the money which my friend Dori gave me for anything other than for what she gave it to me for. I had one belief. As I was alone and didn't have family, I thought earning friends in life was a greater achievement than earning money and saving money. So I used to blow up all of my money on my friends. But gradually, I understood that they were using me. They would ask me to fill petrol in their cars. This was very expensive and sometimes they would borrow as much as Rs 20,000-Rs 30,000, but they never thought to pay me back. Once, I was broke. There wasn't any money in my account. I had just two hundred rupees left in my account. I had to give my rent but didn't have money, so I called all those friends to whom I had given money. They all said that they didn't have a penny and gave me lots of reasons and excuses as to why they could not return me my money in my hour of need. Finally they said sorry and that they couldn't help.

Now there was one normal friend I had. I asked him to keep my things in his house. He wanted to know why. I told him, I had to return to the UK suddenly, and would he take care of my stuff until I returned. I didn't have the nerve to tell him what a fool I was, I had lent all my money and now could not pay my rent. That I was homeless. I told him, 'My dad and mom are calling me. I have to go for sometime.' This friend kept all my luggage. I walked out of my apartment and did not know where to go. The landlord was calling me. I told him to give me two weeks because I was not in Delhi. I still had the house key but I did not dare to go home. So I slept in the bus station for two days. Then, my friend Dori called me and said, 'Happy New Year. I have sent some money to your account. Hope things are going well.' I wished her back. Suddenly tears fell from my eyes and I said, 'Thank you so much Dori. This year is going to be very nice for me.'

After this incident, I stopped giving money to any friends and changed my cell number and disconnected from my rich friends. Somehow, there used to be only one friend who knew my story. One day, he invited me to a pub. It had been a long time since I had gone to a pub. He met me and then said, 'Oh! Shit man. I have forgotten my purse.' He then asked me, 'Could you help me today? I'm getting late to pick up my girlfriend and her friend.' I just looked at him but couldn't refuse, so I filled fuel in his car and went to the pub with his girlfriend and friend.

I was drinking in the bar and they were sitting at the table. Suddenly I heard, 'I stay with Basu because he doesn't have family. No home, so I help him a lot. Sometime for accommodation and food. Many a time, I help him with his education too. Well... he is a self-made man, but he can't earn that much money to survive, because he is an undergraduate.' When I heard this, I felt sad again. So, after a few minutes, when they called me to their table, I said, 'I'm not interested in sitting at that table with you all.' They came to the bar and sat around me. I was in the middle. The bill came. I slid the bill towards my friend and told the waiter, 'He is the guy who will pay because I'm a poor, homeless and orphan guy. If he wasn't there, I would have died long time ago.' My friend gave me a really strange look and said, 'Hey buddy, what happened? I think you've got the wrong idea and drank too much.' I was tipsy, so I smiled at him and said, 'No man! For the first time I got the right idea about you. Oh! Yah. What were you saying? That you are my God? I'm a very poor guy. That's true, but I never thought that you would use my feelings for you to impress the girls. Impressing a girl is really a different thing, but being honest in friendship is an unique thing, buddy. One more thing. You were also talking about status. I'm proud of myself. Whatever I am today, that's all my effort and fight. See my skivvy, it cost Rs 225, my jeans Rs 4,500. My T-shirt cost Rs 1,200, my shoes, it's company is W.....d and it cost Rs 5,000, and I have done really hard work to buy all these things. What about you? Whatever you have put on, it's not yours. All that came from your family's money... Your status is very low before me. Oh! Yes. You were trying to impress these girls, right? You listen to me Ma'am. No offense, but whatever the bill here for your drinks and the pub, I'm paying it all because your boyfriend doesn't have that much money in his pocket. Your boyfriend said I'm a poor guy, right?' I scoffed and walked out of the pub and got back home. After that I never spoke to any of my friends.

I didn't have any Indian friends. All relationships came to an end and I never wanted to make any close friend again. Yet, I still had one friend. He was an Anglo-Indian. I knew the family. They were two brothers. They too used me but they were not so rich. These brothers were not educated but they used to come to my house and invite me on Christmas to their home. I would go to their house and meet their father. I would also visit their relatives with these brothers. Some of them were from Allahabad. The father was very fond of me because I came from so far, struggling all my life and he would ask his children to learn something from my life. As I used to go to their family on every Christmas, I fell in love with Anne, my friends' cousin. I was very close to her, we used to laugh and had fun but I did not ever dare tell her all that was in my heart.

I was very friendly with another cousin of theirs. His name was Ricky. He was a state-level boxer from Uttar Pradesh. He was really fond of me, so whenever I used to go from Delhi to Allahabad, we used to get drunk together. So one time, on Christmas, I decided to tell the girl how I felt. I went out one day with her brothers and cousins, Cyrus and Ricky and Kennedy, and we got drunk. I wanted to get very drunk because I had to propose to this girl. So after getting drunk completely, I asked my friend Kennedy to get one tequila bottle. He asked me why? I told him, 'I am going to propose to Anne today and I need courage, so you do one thing. Just stand at the corner and I'll go to her and try to propose to her. If I cannot, I'll come to you again and have a drink. Then I will run back to her to propose.' He said, 'You are mad. Just go and tell her, that's it.' I smiled at him and said, 'You don't understand. This has been something really bothering me. I'm man but I don't have the nerve to say anything. So, please do whatever I'm saying and help me.' He said, 'Okay then. Let's go.'

I went to this girl's home and called her out. She came out and I told her, 'You see, I would like to tell you something.' She smiled and told me, 'You are drunk.' I replied, 'No. I'm not drunk enough. But I'm drunk so as to have the nerve to say something to you.' She had a smile on her face and asked me again to tell her soon, whatever I wanted to tell her. I ran towards my friend, he had the bottle of booze. I had told him earlier that if I lacked courage, I would come to him for a swig. My girl thought I was crazy, because I had run three times to my friend. The fourth time, my tequila bottle was already finished. I had drunk fast and suspected that my friend, hiding, had also drunk from it. Instead of proposing to her, I asked Anne to give me a hug and whispered in her ear that, 'I love you so much... do you love me?' She smiled back and said, 'Yes.' So I ran back to my friends and I danced a jig and got drunk till I fell down. I went back to Delhi and we started to have long love talks over the telephone. One day, during our conversation, she suddenly asked me one question, 'Hey sweetheart, do you really love me?' I was surprised by the question and I asked her, 'What sort of question is that? I love you, that's why I'm talking to you and that's why I proposed to you, isn't it?' She then said, 'If you love me, then come and speak with my family and ask for my hand.' I felt dead because she was talking like a crazy woman. We were just kids. Of course, not ready to get married. But after thinking for a while, I said, 'If you are talking and testing me and my love, I will definitely come to talk to your family.' After getting off the phone, I began to think, how to go and meet her family and tell them what? I knew that I didn't have any house, no family, so how would this work out? These things knocked at my head again and again.

I booked a train ticket and travelled to Allahabad. The whole night I couldn't sleep on the train because I didn't still know how I was really going to do this. I had read in a book that love is blind and you do a lot of stupid things which you shouldn't be doing. Since I had given her my word and promised her my life and I believed that the man who could not keep his word was no man, I didn't know, what price I would have to pay to keep my word. I reached her home and rang the door bell. I was lucky that they knew me, because I had been to her home to celebrate Christmas with my Anglo-Indian friends. I wished her father, 'Hello! Sir!' He said hello back, but it wasn't Christmas.

He asked me why I was there? I said, 'Well...there are many things in life which we can't decide alone. As you are an adult and you have taken many serious decision in life, I was wondering if you would help me decide something very serious in my life. I want to share this with you and want to know what is right and what is wrong. After all, I'm just a child who always takes decisions on my own. It's better to get help from elders, so that I don't take any wrong decision.' He did not understand what I was trying to say. I had on a nice white shirt, black tie and a smile on my face.

After he said, 'Alright, I'll help you,' I smiled and said, 'You know about me a little bit, right?' He said, 'Yes. last time, your friend told me your story. So I know about you.' I told him, 'Well... I don't have a home, that's true. No family but I'm very capable of solving problems and my surviving all odds is witness to this. I am not going back to my difficult past. I'm going to do something really good. About getting a home, I'm working hard to make my life. And soon I'll have that too. So, what do you think about me? Am I a nice guy?' He really didn't have a clue as to what I was leading up to. He liked what he heard.

He said, 'You are a nice guy, I like you.' After he said this, I got a little more courage to talk and I said, 'See, your daughter Anne. We love each other, so I was thinking... if you felt good about our relationship, I would like to know.' His expression changed. For a while he just stared at my face and then said, 'How dare you think about this? Even if it were possible, where would you keep my daughter? So make one house, one car and two hundred thousand rupees in your account and then come to me. Maybe my mind will change.'

But unluckily, Anne's mother had heard the conversation and she just charged at me and started to abuse me. 'You son of...., how could you think about this? You are such a shameless jerk, to have the guts to come here and talk this shit.' Oh! My...I never expected such humiliation in my life. She called all her Anglo-Indian relatives about and I was soon surrounded by people, all family members and friends, all abusing me. Suddenly one of Anne's uncles produced a shot gun. He had a long moustache and a pony-tail and was fond of hunting. He said, 'Where is the bastard gone, I will shoot him right away.' This time, somewhere I lost my fear.

I was back to my orphanage days. I shouted back at him, 'Hey! If you have the balls, then shoot me, don't just talk, talking doesn't work. What sort of savage and uncivilised people are you all? I came here to just talk and in a very gentlemanly way, but you guys are humiliating me in such a mean way. If I were a bad person, I would have never come to make this proposal, instead I would have hidden it and had fun with your daughter. She wanted to get married to me. I would have done a court marriage. Then what would you have done after that?' I talked in this manner as somewhere, my street upbringing came to the fore. It was as if people had surrounded me to kill me. So I was no longer gentle, I was back in the street eighteen years ago, a street child. People were now quiet. The next day, Anne's mother took me to her cousin, the state-level boxing champion. She took me to get me beaten, but somehow he knew about our love affair, but he had never let me know that he had known. We used to attend barbecue parties together and get drunk, so we were good friends. Anne's mom wanted him to beat me up and tried to convince him that I was wrong. Her cousin was on my side and said, 'How are you're talking to him aunty? He is a nice boy. Look at him, how nicely he is talking to you. He didn't do any mistake for which you are blaming him only. Even your daughter also has to be blamed. Emotion and love are natural things and how nice he is. He came a long way to discuss this matter. That makes him a wise man and your daughter would have fallen in love anyway. If it wasn't Basu, it would have been someone else.' I was happy that someone was on my side. After that I got out of that place, I was very sad because I was very humiliated. I also felt sad that Anne had not come to intervene on my behalf in the conversation. Her older uncle, Henry, had also tried to explain to everyone that Basu had told him of his love for Anne, and that he had known of this affair. He said he had found it was normal, and had not taken it as if the earth had fallen. Basu was a nice and gentle boy. That he had come to confront the family, that's what a wise man does. But to no avail.

After that, I returned to Delhi. My spirit was low. I began to recall the good times I had with Anne. She was tall and I was short. She would call me and say, 'Hey Basu can I put on heels today?' I would smile. I was darker than her and she would rag me about that too. We were always pulling each other's legs. Then one day, she called. I told her I was not going to talk to her any more. She had not come to stand by my side, when I faced the wrath of her parents. If your loved one is not beside you in times of trouble, what kind of love is that? I told her that I had had a good time with her. 'I have already paid a big price for your love.' I asked her a question but she didn't have any answer. Then I told her, 'you can call me back when you have that answer. I don't have any complaint about our relationship because whatever has to happen, it will happen and life is a journey. Your platform has already come and I have to go a long way to my destination.'

৵০৪৫৩

Inspiration Worldwide

Being an orphan, a fighter and a gang member, a survivor, a beggar, a thief, a rag picker, a pick pocket, a domestic servant, a campaigner marching in step with presidents and ministers of many countries, a part of the ILO convention 182 and 138. I had lived the life of the son of the richest man, a five star life and as a pauper, I had struggled in the world of BPOs and I had been an unsuccessful lover. All these myriad experiences shaped me and the book which I have been writing. The book has helped me to cope with my pain, a cathartic exercise. I dream to reach it to my mother — that Mom whom I have never seen. When published, I hope she will read my book and find me.

I don't remember my mother's face. When I recall those

stories which my father told me again and again, and try to refresh my fading memory from what I had written many years ago in the journals I began keeping at the instance of a well-wisher, a fresh wound opens. It compels me to wish to see my mom once before I die. I just want her to hug me as her loved child, instead of an unwanted child. I don't have any complaints against my mother and father, because in life everyone believes in their conviction. My father sacrificed his life for love, because for him, love was life. My mom deserted my dad and me to be famous, and it was her life. Everyone in life is born to be something. They all follow their ways and journeys. I don't have any complaint against my family because at the end, they also had their journeys.

But when I think about meeting my mom again, my heart fills with lots of love for her, rather than any hatred. When I think in this way I feel strange, because the person who gave me birth and brought me in this world, I don't know that person. The heart and the mind always keep wondering and want to learn this hidden truth. But it's okay. Probably this wound will never heal, but I can understand the love between mother and son, the love among family and the word just known as 'love' itself. The person who values food most is the one who has been starving for ages.

One day, about two years ago, in 2012, I received a call

from Kailash Satyarthiji. As usual, he asked me, 'How's life and what are you doing nowadays?' Most times, it would be I who called him. And I would be drunk. He did not know that. This time, he wanted to visit my institute, known as the American and British Institute of Lingua Franca. My visitors were two beautiful foreign girls along with Kailashji and his wife Sumedhaji. When they came visiting, I showed them how I was running my institute. Kailashji was really impressed with what I was doing.

After this meeting, around two week later, Kailashji called me again. He asked me to come to his home this time. It had been quite some time since I had visited him. So, this time, I decided to go to see him. He asked me about my plans and I told him that I had written a book and I wanted to get it published. He said, 'I'll help you to the best of my ability to get it published.' I was very happy and I went with him to his home. He read my draft with a lot of interest and gave some valuable suggestions. He also spoke with potential publishers for this purpose. He introduced me to Renuji of Vitasta. I stayed with Kailashji for a few days.

Kailashji and Sumedhaji treat me as their son. I have stayed with them at their residence many a times as family. I have always been concerned about his health owing to his hectic schedule round the year. Whenever I used to visit Kailashji, I used to give him health tips and take him for morning walks compulsorily. Kailashji was also concerned about my health and well being and particularly in the wake of the ugly episode at my English training institute, he asked me to stay at Mukti Ashram. Subsequently he asked Bachpan Bachao Andolan's officers to help me out. They, in turn, asked me to begin helping in coordination with the international volunteers, along with another staff member, Jubil Lalung.

I gave up teaching English and joined the Bachpan Bachao Andolan.

Later on, I was vested with the full responsibility of the work of the international volunteer coordination. I kept living in Mukti Ashram and progressed with my book as well. Groups of volunteer students used to frequently visit Mukti Ashram, Bal Ashram — the long-term rehabilitation centre of Bachpan Bachao Andolan at Virat Nagar near Jaipur in Rajasthan. These groups also went on field visits for weeks together, to understand the issue of child labour and how BBA tackles it with child-friendly villages and meaningful engagement with the youth. These visits were truly enriching for me as well. At Mukti Ashram, sometimes, I had to work on children's case studies, do counseling and spend time with them so that they could tide over their hardship. I also had to call all the students, professors and foreigners from across the world and host the interns and the volunteers.

I knew that I couldn't bring any great change in

society but I also knew that if my book got published, it could change many things. At least people would be able to read about the life a street child had and the suffering he underwent. This knowledge could change people's mind towards street children and child labour. I first got a volunteers' team to host some child labourers. Then I made a presentation on child labour and issues of children's rights. People were listening to me very carefully and at that moment, I thought that I could change people's mentality with opportunities like this.

Those volunteer students were the future of the world and if I could make the world aware of the future of the world, then the problem would be solved. But when I really explored the circumstances of these volunteer students, they were just freshers, students who really wanted to travel the world and get experience. They didn't have any idea about the life they were themselves living. They didn't like the lives they were living, they felt that they didn't have anything in life. In reality, these student volunteers couldn't share anything with their parents because the parents were too busy making money. They had forgotten that their children needed values, love, sharing and Dad's time. The children were a heartbroken lot, when boyfriends left them, they were sad, if girlfriends left them they were sad. They were totally tangled in such complex emotional problems and this made their lives more complicated.

When I asked them, 'what do you do for your fun?', they would say, go to a pub and get drunk. I asked them another question, what they would like to be in the future? They didn't have any answer but all of them had similar replies — that they were still thinking and trying to figure out what to do. It was very easy for me to understand their lifestyle because I had spent many years trying to understand the way people lived. When I started to meet the volunteers personally, they began to share their personal problems like family problem, boyfriend and girlfriend problem with me. So, when I got lots of similar stories, then I came up with the idea that I would share my story with these volunteers. When I shared my story, I definitely got hurt in the process of recollection. I was scratching my old wounds and, of course, it still bled. But my memory had been fading. As I began to share my story with others as an adult, scenes came alive and the story began to touch these students.

I told them that yesterday was history. It could be a happy time or a bad time. Learn from it. Tomorrow is a mystery. You don't know what's going to happen. Just plan and work along that plan. But don't forget my dears, today is the gift which you have got. Now think about how you are going to live, treat this as your last day and live life. Smile, make others smile, help the needy, love your mom, dad and value your friends who respect you, then see how life treats you. Because today is the party and you are going to dance like mad. Don't think about doing a right step, for you every step is right. Just dance. In our lives, we are all concerned about the right step but you never know, whatever step you feel is wrong could be the right step too. So don't try to understand too much what others feel, judge and how others react. That's not important because it's hard to x-ray someone's mind and if you try to go according to what others think, you will never dare to begin any action in life. You would care what other people think and what would be another's reaction. Only one thing you need to understand and that is, you and your belief in yourself. Value those things you have, whether it is little or much. Just make something beautiful out if it.

With such principles that I really followed in my own life, I managed to bring smiles to my student volunteers' faces. After they returned to their schools and colleges, I received a lot of postcards and mails that said my story had changed their lives. They said, they had begun to hug their Moms and Dads daily, because at least, they had a family. Now they valued their resources more than ever before and were serious about life. They felt comfortable and alive, they were comparing my life with their lives and valuing themselves. That, how lucky they are to have families and were content with what they had. When I read these postcards, I cried in my room. It was easy to cry in my room because I could not cry in front of other people. I was also pleasantly surprised! I didn't know that pain could solve the problems of pain, and give other people a chance to understand life.

When I realised that my story could help bring positivity in someone's life, I didn't stop sharing my story. Students began to say that my story was inspirational. Then I realised that somehow, my past had helped inspire many young people and they wanted to do something right. I still remember the day when I was making a presentation to one group which came from Babson College (USA) at Bal Ashram. A professor accompanying the group, Elizabeth, raised her hand and asked me a question, 'From where did you complete your education?' I was in the middle of the presentation. I didn't understand what answer I should be giving her. I thought I had said something wrong in the presentation. I told her, 'You guess Ma'am, from where I must have done my education.' She thought for a moment and said, 'Maybe, America or the UK.' I smiled and felt relaxed that there was nothing wrong with my presentation. Then I asked this lady, 'Why you felt that?' She said, 'Your English has the native speaker touch, that's why.' Now, at this time, I suddenly recalled my days of teaching English to Indians and how hard it was for me to educate myself.

There was the day when I first came to Kailashji's organisation as a runaway child. They gave non-formal education to all the children in their rehabilitation centre. I didn't know Hindi. I could read and write in English only. But they couldn't send me to any private English medium school because that would have been discrimination against other children. With the limited resources that Bachpan Bachao Andolan had, it always strived to help as many children as it possibly could at Mukti Ashram and Bal Ashram by sending them to nearby schools.

I would collect the English books and keep reading and I would ask people who came to visit for a book in English. I was very good in the martial arts and wanted to pursue it further. Mukti Ashram had arranged for my martial arts training for some time during my stay before 2005.

Post 2005, I started to teach martial art to others and saved some money. This is how I managed to reach the 3rd level of the art. When I was promoted to the 4th grade of school, I fought with a bully boy and somehow I beat him a lot. My rehabilitation director thought I was a very dangerous guy for the transition school. So I had to get out of even this transition school. After that, I saved more money and and I sat for the 7th grade examination. I was selected and got the first position in the entire school. Then came some provisions by the Government of India that children who could not for some reason go to formal schools could complete their education by enrolling with the National Institute of Open Schooling. So I enrolled here and completed my high school-level education.

Now the problem was that I had jumped grades a lot and my confidence was low. Then I met my friend, Dori Santolaya. She was a very nice lady. When she asked me what I was doing, I told her, 'I have jumped a lot and I don't know whether I'm capable of competing with regular children. I want to go to an expensive school where rich people's children study.' Dori understood my quest for higher education at a 'good' institution and told me that she would like to help me with my higher studies and within a few months, I got admission in the Joseph and Mary Senior Secondary School. Here I was selected as school captain within a month. All the teachers and administration department of the school became my friends and I realised that I was not bad in my studies too. I gave my senior secondary examination, again from the National Institute of Open Schooling.

After this, I wanted to get admission in an university. They said, 'You don't have mom and dad's name. That field is mandatory in the forms to be to filled.' For a year, I struggled to get enrolled in a college. Finally, I managed to meet the vice-chancellor of the university. He too said, he could not admit me as I did not know my parent's name. Then I told him that, 'Sir, do you know my father's name?' He said, 'No.' So I smiled and told him, 'So, just write NA or XX. The Computer will accept. If you don't know my father's name and even I don't know his name, so how will the computer know?' This gentleman smiled at me and told the Registrar to give me admission. I couldn't go to a regular college but I had an enrollment in Delhi University and I appeared for the examinations. I couldn't attend a single lecture of any professor at any of its colleges, but I graduated from Delhi University after writing its examination.

Thinking about how I had educated myself, I smiled at Elizabeth and told her, 'I'll tell you the whole story of my life after this presentation, is that okay with you?' She smiled and said, 'Okay.' So after the presentation, we met and I told her my story. She couldn't believe that I had faced such hardships in life. She hugged me and said, 'keep it up. Keep inspiring people because I can see that my students were listening to you very carefully and found your presentation inspirational. They never listen to me like that.' Then we laughed and moved to have a cup of tea.

During my stint as a volunteer coordinator at Bachpan Bachao Andolan, I was blessed to have kept meeting many university professors and students from across the world. Once, I had to host three volunteers from Sweden. They were daughters of very big businessmen. Escorting them, I had the opportunity to meet Dileep Baid, an entrepreneur in the state of Rajasthan. When I went to his home, he welcomed the three girls and he also treated me like a foreigner. Then he asked me where I was from. I answered, I'm from India. He then wanted to know more about me. We sat for a while and he started to ask me a lot of questions. He also talked about his own struggle in the business world. When I told him my story, he listened to me with rapt attention and wished me all the best.

There was a programme known as 'Leader's Quest' which was interviewing Dileep Baid. In that programme he shared my story with his audience. After that, Dileepji's daughter, Anubha, who soon became a friend, suggested that I should be interviewed by 'Leader's Quest'. It occurred to me then that it was a programme for leaders, and CEOs. If I got an opportunity to speak at this forum, I could meet many people who could help our movement. The CEOs had reached the zenith of achievement. I came from the grass-root. My story could give the programme an extra dimension.

I was working for Bachpan Bachao Andolan (Save the Childhood Movement). I decided to involve the founder, Kailashji. I asked Leader Quest to contact him too. Leader Quest convinced Kailashji and soon he was on board. Kailashji was invited as the keynote speaker at POW WOW at Samode Palace in Jaipur in September 2013. As planned, a group of leaders from the Quest visited Bal Ashram and spent the entire day with the Children. Kailashji explained all about the struggles of child labourers and street children, the UN and ILO policies and Convention 182 and 138.

When it was my turn, I told the CEOs and leaders my story, which you have been reading in this book. Many of them could not control their tears and a coordinator named Jayma hugged me. I felt very warm because I was very sad. I was sad, I had been scratching my old wounds to gain support for our cause. But there was another man, a tall guy full of life and smile, a very charming person, who was very interested in my story and took keen interest in all that I did. He took interest in the idea of a book, and one day he offered to sponsor my book. He told me he had discussed my life and my book with several people and one person had wanted to know, where could she get this book.

This book was my dream. I had hope that I would meet my mom again, through this book. I don't know what she must be doing in some corner of this world. If she is a super model now, she will be able to read this book. However, this book is equally important for people to know the situation of tiny four-year-old children who beg, pick rags, live on the streets all over the world. How a journey begins, how the story of survival plays out. A story to be shared with the world.

After this book, I plan to join acting school, which is a childhood dream. As a successful actor, I plan to take care of twenty-five orphan children. They will have a big and nice house where they will wake up with music in the morning. There'd be remote-controlled curtains and their attendant would serve them juice, before they get out of bed. They will have all those facilities which the child of a country's president has. I will get them foster parents and sponsors who would be great actors and tycoons. They will talk to these children as their parents. I feel that everyone's dream comes true, once you dare to dream. There is the saying, 'The first step to succeed is to dare to take the first step itself.'

The next thing would be to see how my life will pan out after this book is published.

ත♋ත♋